A Letter From General Secretary Leonid I. Brezhnev

ПОСЕТИТЕЛЯМ ВЫСТАВКИ ШЕДЕВРОВ ЖИВОПИСИ
ИЗ МУЗЕЕВ СОВЕТСКОГО СОЮЗА

Я рад возможности приветствовать американских посетителей выставки произведений живописи из коллекции крупнейших музеев Советского Союза – Государственного Эрмитажа и Государственного Русского музея.

Эта выставка является одним из проявлений достигнутого за последние годы улучшения отношений между Союзом Советских Социалистических Республик и Соединенными Штатами Америки, свидетельством растущего интереса американского и советского народов к истории и культуре обеих стран.

Выставка открывается в год, когда народы мира отмечают тридцатилетие победоносного завершения второй мировой войны, в которой советский и американский народы боролись против общего врага. Наши страны не могут забыть уроков прошлой войны, они должны всеми силами содействовать установлению мира и сотрудничества между народами.

Вот почему Коммунистическая партия Советского Союза, наше Правительство считают необходимым поддерживать и развивать все виды сотрудничества, которые служат укреплению взаимопонимания и взаимного уважения между народами.

Мы с удовлетворением отмечаем расширение культурных связей между нашими странами, а также плодотворную инициативу д-ра Арманда Хаммера, который существенно способствовал организации настоящей выставки.

Мы убеждены, что сокровища Эрмитажа и Русского музея вызовут искренний интерес американского зрителя и послужат общему делу упрочения советско-американских отношений.

Л. БРЕЖНЕВ

TO THE VISITORS OF THE EXHIBITION OF MASTER PAINTINGS FROM MUSEUMS OF THE SOVIET UNION

I am glad to take this opportunity to greet American visitors of the exhibition of paintings from the collection of the largest museums of the Soviet Union—the State Hermitage and the State Russian Museum.

This exhibition represents one of the manifestations of the improvement in relations between the Union of Soviet Socialist Republics and the United States of America reached in the recent years and illustrates the growing interest of the American and Soviet peoples towards history and culture of both countries.

The exhibition is opened in the year when the peoples of the world commemorate the 30th Anniversary of the victorious ending of the second World War in which the Soviet and American peoples have fought against the common enemy. Our countries cannot forget the lessons of the last war and with all their strength they have to further establishing peace and cooperation among the peoples.

That is why the Communist Party of the Soviet Union and our Government believe it necessary to support and develop all kinds of cooperation which serve to facilitate the strengthening of mutual understanding and mutual respect among the peoples.

We note with satisfaction the expansion of cultural ties between our countries and also the fruitful initiative of Dr. Armand Hammer who considerably promoted organizing this exhibition.

We believe that the treasures of the Hermitage and the Russian Museum will excite a genuine interest of the American audience and contribute to the common cause of strengthening the Soviet-American relations.

L. Brezhnev

Master Paintings from The Hermitage and The State Russian Museum

Leningrad

Edited by John Richardson and Eric Zafran

Master
Paintings
from
The Hermitage
and
The State
Russian Museum
Leningrad

National Gallery of Art, Washington, D.C.
M. Knoedler & Co., Inc., New York, N.Y.
The Detroit Institute of Arts, Detroit, Michigan
Los Angeles County Museum of Art, Los Angeles, California
The Museum of Fine Arts, Houston, Houston, Texas

1975-1976

This exhibition has been designated an official event by the American
Revolution Bicentennial Administration.

frontispiece: Louis Le Nain, *A Visit to Grandmother* (detail of No. 8), The Hermitage.

Introduction

In the present exhibition the State Hermitage Museum presents the American public with selected treasures of western European painting from its collection for the second time. But, whereas the first exhibition, which travelled around the United States in 1973, was limited to French Impressionists and Post-Impressionists, the present exhibition represents a much wider range, embracing as it does some five hundred years of painting in eight countries of western Europe. Masterpieces by Poussin and Picasso, Caravaggio and Tiepolo, Rubens and Velázquez, Rembrandt and Hals and many other great painters are included.

Never before has such a representative exhibition left the walls of the Hermitage to be shown abroad.

The State Hermitage Museum is a repository of works of art of various nations and epochs from primitive periods up to the present time, but the oldest and most significant part of the huge museum is the collection of western European art. This ranks among the first in the world not only by virtue of the number of paintings but also because of their high quality.

The art collection of the Hermitage dates back to the first quarter of the eighteenth century when the first paintings were acquired in the reign of Peter the Great. Later in the century the acquisition by the museum of such famous private art collections as those of Count Brühl from Dresden, Baron Crozat, the Duc de Choiseul and Comte de Baudoin from Paris, Sir Robert Walpole from England and many others put the Hermitage among the finest art galleries in the world. About half the western European paintings shown in the present exhibition come from the collections named above: *Dead Christ with the Virgin Mary and an Angel* by Veronese, *Maecenas Presenting the Arts to Augustus* by Tiepolo, *Portrait of an Actor* by Fetti, both canvases by Rembrandt, *Portrait of a Man* by Hals, *A Forest Marsh* by Ruisdael, *A Family Group* by Van Dyck, *Landscape With a Wagon* by Rubens, *Boy with a Dog* by Murillo, *The Repast* by Velázquez, *A Visit to Grandmother* by Le Nain, *Tancred and Erminia* by Poussin.

During the first half of the nineteenth century works of art continued to flow into the museum. The acquisition, in 1814, of a major part of the collection from Malmaison, belonging to the Empress Josephine, Napoleon's first wife, deserves special mention. In the present exhibition this collection is represented by Claude Lorrain's *Landscape with the Rest on the Flight into Egypt*. It was only at the end of the century that there was a sharp decrease in the acquisition of paintings by the gallery.

The collections of the Hermitage had been formed as a palace museum and, therefore, reflected to a considerable extent the tastes of its founders, the Imperial family. Thus, by the eve of the October Revolution of 1917, certain important schools and periods of art, which should be included in any great museum, were either represented inadequately or not represented at all. To remedy this, major acquisitions were made after the Revolution from important private collections and noblemen's palaces which had been nationalized. The number of works of art acquired in post-revolutionary years was fantastic. These acquisitions not only complemented but changed the entire character of the old sections of the Gallery. They also helped to create new sections, for instance the very fine collection of Impressionist and Post-Impressionist paintings.

By representing all schools in the department of painting—Italian, French, Spanish, Flemish, Dutch, German and English—the choice of works in the present exhibition is intended to reflect the special riches of the Hermitage collection. For instance, Italian painting is represented here mainly by works of the seventeenth and eighteenth centuries and not by earlier periods, because the Hermitage is especially rich in the former field.

French art, on the other hand, is represented by both old masters and twentieth century works. Other schools of western European painting are shown in the present exhibition in proportion to their representation in the Museum's collections.

Academician B. Piotrovsky
Director of State Hermitage

Treasures from Leningrad

by Denys Sutton

Leningrad is most beautiful in winter when snow invests the city with a poetical quality, at least in the eyes of the romantic traveler; but even in summer it possesses its own special charm. The white nights are famous, and Madame Vigée-Lebrun, who came to Russia in 1795, claimed that they made the palaces on the Neva look like ancient temples. As well as delighting the eye, the city touches the hearts of those who love Pushkin and Dostoevsky and who enjoy the grand tradition of Russian opera, ballet and theatre. It is a city that brings the visitor close to the center of Russian history, and the experience of seeing the art treasures in the Hermitage and the Russian State Museum is an exhilarating one.

The charm and distinction of the architecture is unforgettable. The brilliantly colored buildings by Bartolomeo Rastrelli, the elegant facade of the Academy of Arts designed by Vallin de la Mothe, the contributions of Giacomo Quarenghi and Carlo Rossi, and the achievements of such local architects as A. P. Kokorinov and I. Y. Starov, are a continual pleasure—so is the Winter Palace (fig. 1) the most intriguing architectural complex in Leningrad.

Nearby the city the handsome palaces of Tsarskoye Selo, Peterhof, and Pavlosk reflect an amazing variety of styles and attest to the sureness of taste of Russia's rulers. Only at Tsarskoye Selo and Pavlosk is it possible to appreciate the genius of Charles Cameron, that elegant master of the neo-classic style that linked Western Europe, Russia and the United States. It is also significant that the famous *Mir Iskusstva* (World of Art) movement, founded by Diaghilev and Alexandre Benois, originated in St. Petersburg; for its title evokes the ethos of a city which has rejoiced in the arts ever since its foundation by Peter the Great in 1703.

How appropriate that the majestic equestrian statue of this Tsar, which Catherine the Great commissioned from Etienne-Maurice Falconet, should face the River Neva. It serves as a reminder that Peter the Great was eager to bring his country into closer contact with the West. He was the only Russian ruler of the eighteenth century to visit Paris, the artistic heart of Europe, until Paul I went there, as the "Comte du Nord," before his accession to the throne.

Peter the Great has not perhaps received sufficient credit for his efforts to enrich Russian culture. It is the Empress Catherine who invariably occupies the center of the stage. Yet Peter was the virtual founder of the Hermitage. He purchased a great many paintings including one of the finest Rembrandts in Russia, *David's Farewell to Jonathan*. He also acquired the famous marble, *Venus of Taurida,* a Roman copy after a Greek original.

Ever since boyhood Peter had been interested in collecting weapons, coins, and medals, and in 1714 he established a *Kunstkammer*, which contained botanical, zoological, and mineral items as well as curiosities and works of art. In 1715 Alexei Demidov, who had vast interests in Siberia, sent him twenty ancient gold objects that had been discovered in a *kurgan* (burial mound) on one of his estates, while the following year, M. P. Gagarin, Governor of Tobolsk, sent him fifty-six similar gold objects. And in 1718 the government decreed the"collecting from earth and water of old inscriptions, ancient weapons, dishes, and everything old and unusual." Hence the collection of Scythian art treasures, which was recently introduced to the American public by the Metropolitan Museum of Art.

In 1715 this Tsar also arranged for a group of French artists, architects, and craftsmen to come to St. Petersburg to embellish the city. One of this contingent was J. B. A. Leblond, who was charged with the task of working out a master-plan, and to him is due the two great prospects that radiate from the Admiralty. He also worked at Peterhof, where Nicolas Pineau designed the panelling in the Tsar's study at Monplaisir, and where Philippe Pillement decorated the Great Hall with a charming ceiling in the manner of Berain. Less successful were the Tsar's efforts to persuade J. M. Nattier and J. B. Oudry to come to Russia: he had to settle for a minor French painter, Louis Caravague. However, when Peter and his wife, Catherine I, were in France they sat for Nattier; these portraits are now in the Hermitage. On a subsequent visit to Paris in 1717, Peter was delighted when the Duc d'Antin, at the behest of Louis XV, presented him with two series of Gobelins tapestries (now in the Hermitage), as he was eager to establish a tapestry workshop in St. Petersburg.

The eighteenth century was a period of considerable economic and cultural expansion in Russia, and sustained efforts were made by Peter's successors to foster relations with the West. The Empress Anna Ivanovna was not a patrically enthusiastic art lover—she was more interested in brightly colored clothes, gambling, and the theatre— nevertheless she imposed on her court some of the Western European graces.

fig. 2. The Ambassadors' Staircase by B. Rastrelli, reconstructed after the fire of 1837 by V. P. Stasov. Watercolor by K. A. Ukhtomsky, 1860. Courtesy Aurora Editions, Leningrad.

Treasures from Leningrad

During the reign of the Empress Elizabeth, the younger daughter of Peter the Great, St. Petersburg became the capital of Russia and a center of artistic activity. Elizabeth had an instinctive sense of quality and the taste to find the architects and artisans who were to give this city its cosmopolitan character. She was especially lucky in her principal architect, Bartolomeo Rastrelli, whose father, Carlo, had also worked in Russia. Bartolomeo put his stamp on St. Petersburg; he evolved his own style—a mixture of the Baroque and Rococo—that also owed something to Russia's past. This debt may be seen in Smolny Cathedral, which reflects the influence of Russian medieval architecture.

Rastrelli designed the Summer Palace—a wooden edifice, now no more, though its appearance is recorded in a charming print by Makhyev—but his masterpiece was the Winter Palace, formerly the chief residence of the Imperial family and now the Hermitage Museum. Five other palaces preceded it, and many changes have occurred to the building since 1754-62. As it now stands, it offers a history of the main phases in Leningrad's architectural development, from the mid-eighteenth century to the mid-nineteenth century, with interior and exterior contributions by foreign and Russian architects and designers. Successively, in fact, Baroque, Rococo, Neo-Classicism and Eclectism made their mark on the Winter Palace; the buildings added to Rastrelli's structure comprise the Little Hermitage, the Old Hermitage, and the Hermitage Theatre in the eighteenth century, and the New Hermitage in the nineteenth.

One of the charms of the Winter Palace is its variety. Visitors have the impression that they are being led through a succession of Aladdin's caves; they are also constantly reminded of episodes in Russian history. For sheer magnificence one need but cite such splendid interiors as the Malachite Room (fig. 4), the Concert Hall and the Military Gallery. The last-mentioned has a special appeal for lovers of *War and Peace,* for in this gallery, which was designed by Rossi in 1826— six small rooms were demolished to make way for it—hang 332 portraits of generals who served in the 1812 Franco-Russian War and the 1813-14 campaign. The portraits were painted by the English artist, George Dawe, with the assistance of the Russian painters, A. V. Polyakov and V. A. Golikov.

The appearance of this gallery is recorded in a delightful painting by G. Chernetsov of 1827 which shows officers inspecting the portraits. The atmosphere of other interiors in the Hermitage has been effectively captured by nineteenth century painters; two of the most evocative records are of the Armorial Hall by A. Ladurner, of 1838, and the St. George's Hall by K. Ukhtomsky, of 1862 (fig. 3). These works remind us that the Hermitage, like the Louvre, was originally a palace, and the note of pomp and circumstance is unquestionably sounded when visitors mount the Ambassadors' staircase (fig. 2). This was designed by Quarenghi and partly reconstructed and remodelled by V. P. Stasov after the disastrous fire of 1837 which reduced the building to a charred skeleton.

One powerful influence in determining the character of the Hermitage collection has been the long and rewarding artistic dialogue between the Russians and the French. The Empress Elizabeth had come to the throne as the result of a palace revolution—eighteenth century St. Petersburg was rife with intrigue—in which the French ambassador, the Marquis de la Chétardie, and her French surgeon, Dr. Armand Lestocq, played a considerable part. This coup had strengthened ties between the two courts. Furthermore Louis XV's advisors thought that the dissemination of French art in Russia would smooth diplomatic relations, and in pursuance of this policy Louis Tocqué, one of the most talented portrait painters in Paris, went to St. Petersburg, where he painted the Empress—a full-length, state portrait of her is in the Hermitage—and members of the court. However, the French were not the only foreign artists active in Russia. Tocqué was upset when he found Pietro Rotari there. This able Venetian painter executed some enchanting portraits of Russian beauties. Jacopo Guarana and Gaspare Diziani also received commissions—to paint decorations for the Winter Palace—and Francesco Fontebasso worked in Russia from 1760 until 1762.

Nevertheless French taste was more or less paramount in Russia. It was a sign of this that Alexei Razoumovsky ordered a vast consignment of wine from France, including several thousand bottles of champagne, and that Mikhail Vorontsov sent the Empress Elizabeth French *pâtés* and truffles from Paris. Vorontsov was so enchanted by Versailles that he had his St. Petersburg residence decorated in the French style. Louis XV gave him furniture and tapestries, but these were lost at sea; subsequently the king dispatched a second set of tapestries.

Another major figure who played an outstanding role in disseminating French culture in Russia was Count Ivan Ivanovich Shuvalov. He became Empress Elizabeth's

fig. 3. St. George's Hall by G. Quarenghi, reconstructed after the fire of 1837. Watercolor by K. A. Ukhtomsky, 1862.

fig. 4. Malachite Room by A. P. Briullov. Watercolor by K. A. Ukhtomsky, 1865.

Treasures from Leningrad

favorite and was nicknamed "Monsieur Pompadour." Shuvalov had as sure an eye as Louis XV's mistress, and was in touch with leading French *philosophes,* such as d'Alembert, Diderot, and Voltaire, whom he supplied with information for his history of Russia under Peter the Great. Shuvalov's interest in intellectual and artistic matters manifested itself when, together with Mikhail Lomonosov, he founded Moscow University. He also became President of the Academy of Arts in St. Petersburg in 1757 and, two years later, brought Vallin de La Mothe to the city to design the imposing building facing the River Neva which formerly housed this institution.

When Empress Elizabeth died in 1762, Peter III came to the throne, but he was deposed a few months later and replaced by his wife. Subsequently known as Catherine the Great, the German-born Empress was a powerful and fascinating figure who made an immense contribution to Russian life. She was a woman of strong character who knew how to get her own way, and play off one personality against another. She was a decided sensualist and chose her lovers with deliberation; some were selected by her one time favorite Prince Potemkin, a noble statesman. She was determined to leave her mark on European culture and transform her court into an intellectual center. She maintained relations with many French men of letters and was devoted to Voltaire. She also resolved to build up an important art collection, and in pursuance of this aim, availed herself of the services of Diderot and Baron Grimm, both of whom visited Russia. Her representative in Paris, Prince D. M. Galitzine, was a shrewd judge of art and a patron of Houdon, who designed tombs for members of his family. This sculptor also made a bust of Catherine (Hermitage), which was commissioned by Count A. S. Stroganov.

Given her vast resources, Catherine was able to secure most of the treasures that were offered to her; for instance, in 1764, when Frederick the Great was in financial difficulties and unable to acquire the collection of paintings which the Prussian dealer, J. E. Gotzkowski, had formed for him, Catherine bought it instead. In 1769 Prince A. P. Beloselsky, Russian Minister in Dresden, reported to St. Petersburg that the estate of the late Count Heinrich von Brühl, who had been Chancellor to Augustus III, Elector of Saxony and King of Poland, was heavily encumbered by debt and that his collection was available. The Empress jumped at her Minister's suggestion, thereby effecting a splendid coup; the Brühl collection was rich in remarkable works—four Rembrandts, five Rubens, two Watteaus, many excellent Dutch landscapes and cabinet pictures, and G. B. Tiepolo's *Maecenas Presenting the Arts to Augustus* (No. 6). The collection also contained an impressive group of drawings.

Prince Galitzine continued to look after Catherine's artistic interests after his transfer to the Netherlands. In 1768, when in Brussels, he secured for her the notable collection of his *cher confrère,* Count Coblentz, the Austrian Minister. This contained five works by Rubens, among other paintings, and some six thousand drawings. By no means all the Empress's acquisitions arrived safely in St. Petersburg: for example, the paintings she bought at the Braankamp sale in Amsterdam in 1771 were lost at sea.

During the 1770's Catherine's appetite for art remained keen. Her Paris agents kept her fully informed about works coming on to the market—Paris auctions were then the best organized—or else they pounced on collections before they came up for public sale. One excellent group of works of art to enter her possession by private treaty belonged to Baron Crozat de Thiers. She secured this in 1772, two years after her purchase of the Tronchin collection. The Crozat collection, one of the most celebrated in France, had been formed by the banker, Pierre Crozat. It numbered some five hundred items and was rich in masterpieces, such as Giorgione's *Judith* (then given to Raphael), Raphael's *Virgin and Child with St. Joseph,* four Veroneses—including the *Dead Christ* (No. 2)—Tintoretto's *St. John the Baptist* and Fetti's brilliant *Actor* (No. 4). In addition, it included admirable works by Rubens and Van Dyck, five Poussins, three Watteaus, and Louis Le Nain's *A Visit to Grandmother* (No. 8).

Feeling was aroused when news of the sale became known in Paris. The Marquis de Marigny, Minister of Arts, was distressed about the sale, and the only picture from the collection to remain in France was Van Dyck's *Portrait of Charles I.* This stayed at the request of Madame du Barry, who claimed that her husband's family was descended from the House of Stuart. (Mrs. 'Jack' Gardner, founder of the museum in Boston that bears her name, nurtured the same belief.) Diderot, who had played a major part in concluding the transaction, shrugged off criticism. "So much the worse for France," he wrote to Falconet, "if we must sell our pictures in time of peace, whereas Catherine can buy them in the middle of a war. Science, art, taste, wisdom are

g. 5. "The Raphael *Loggie*" by B. Quarenghi. Watercolor by K. A. Ukhtomsky, 1860. Courtesy Aurora Editions, Leningrad.

13

traveling northwards and barbarism and all it brings in its train, is coming south."

There was likewise an outburst of indignation in England when, in 1779, the Empress secured the famous collection at Houghton formed by Sir Robert Walpole (first Earl of Orford), Prime Minister to George I and George II. Once again a Russian diplomat was the go-between; in this case, Count Musin-Pushkin, the Russian ambassador in London. Catherine wrote to Baron Grimm (February, 1779) that she was negotiating for the collection. "You see," were her words, "how the birds fly into my snare of their own accord." In April she told the same correspondent: "Your humble servant has got her claws on them (the pictures) and will no more let them go than a cat would a mouse." The Houghton collection was a splendid prize. It contained paintings by Van Dyck, Rubens (No. 16) and Snyders, Poussin and Claude, Salvator Rosa and Luca Giordano. The loss of the collection was understandably lamented by Horace Walpole and provoked a question from John Wilkes in Parliament.

However, Catherine's resources were not endless. The last major collection to enter her collection was that of Comte de Baudouin; negotiations over its purchase dragged on for some years, and she complained that she had no money for its acquisition. Finally in 1784 she bought it for her new favorite, Count A. D. Lanskoy, but he died shortly afterwards, and the pictures entered the Hermitage instead.

Catherine bought modern art as well as old masters, showing a special predilection for the French School. For example, she commissioned Chardin to paint *The Attributes of the Arts* (No. 12). However, she also acquired English paintings—works by William Marlow and Thomas Jones—and she asked Sir Joshua Reynolds to paint a picture of his choice. He selected as his subject *The Infant Hercules Strangling the Serpents,* which was interpreted as symbolizing Russia's growing power. Thomas Banks, the sculptor, also spent a year in St. Petersburg. But the primary English influence in Russia during the eighteenth century was not so much on the arts as on landscape gardening; one Joseph Bush producing the plan for the gardens at Tsarskoye Selo in 1789. English gardens became the rage.

Like many other patrons of the day, Catherine also collected classical art. One of her chief acquisitions in this domain was the group of marbles—mostly portrait busts—which had been formed by Lyde Browne, a director of the Bank of England, who lived at Wimbledon. This cost the Empress £23,000, but the transaction does not appear to have been without problems, and some of Lyde Browne's pieces were later bought by Lord Egremont and Charles Towneley.

Russian collectors soon learned to be wary of false attributions and fakes. Catherine, for instance, told Baron Grimm to inform Reiffenstein, who worked for her in Rome, that he was to buy nothing more from a dealer called Jenkins. "It is scandalous," she said, "to pass off such miserable works as those of well-known artists. We are quite dismayed to see such daubs."

The desire to collect was by no means limited to the crown. The handsome palaces of the Russian nobility in St. Petersburg and elsewhere were adorned with some of the finest examples of French art and craftsmanship, and a patron such as Count Sheremetiev encouraged his serfs to copy French furniture. One especially perceptive collector of Catherine's time was Count A. S. Stroganov, whose family palace, designed by Bartolemeo Rastrelli, has its entrance on the Nevsky Prospect. He was President of the Academy of Arts and opened his collection to the public. Although he acquired works by Hubert Robert, Greuze, and Vernet, he was especially enamored of Italian art and was also a patron of contemporary Russian painters.

Another notable collector, Prince Nicolay Borisovich Yusupov, admired Greuze and Fragonard, also Sèvres porcelain, as witness three services made for him at the Sèvres factory which are now in the Hermitage. Yusupov founded his own porcelain works at his estate, Arkhangeloskoye, where the house was designed by Quarenghi. This talented connoisseur, who was notorious for his love affairs, had one gallery at Arkhangeloskoye and another in his St. Petersburg palace. He was also a patron of Canova, who is well represented in the Hermitage.

By the time the Empress died in 1796, works of art were displayed in three galleries in the Winter Palace— in the Little Hermitage, the Raphael *Loggie* (fig. 5) designed by Quarenghi in 1788, with its copies by H. Unterbergher and other artists after Raphael's famous decorations, and the building now called the Old Hermitage. Permission to see the collections could be obtained from General Betski, Intendant of the Palace Buildings, who had lived for many years in Paris and was devoted to the arts. Students from the Academy of Arts were allowed to copy pictures in the Hermitage.

Although the pace of collecting slackened after

Catherine's death, it did not slow down completely. Foreign artists and architects continued to come to Russia, among them Madame Vigée-Lebrun, a refugee from the French Revolution. She painted many charming portraits and broke into tears when she left the country, where she had spent six happy years.

Alexander I, a keen collector, was fortunate to enjoy the service of an able curator of painting, Labensky. He helped acquire one of Caravaggio's early masterpieces, *The Lute Player* (No. 3) at the sale of the Giustiniani collection in Rome. The agent whom Alexander employed in this and other transactions was Baron Vivant Denon, who had once been *en poste* at St. Petersburg and was one of the most brilliant connoisseurs of his day.

Times of war and social upheaval are always propitious for a collector with funds at his disposal. Alexander took advantage of the situation in France to conclude a deal with Josephine, acquiring thirty-eight pictures from her collection. This had been housed in a special gallery at Malmaison and included Claude's *Landscape with the Rest on the Flight into Egypt* (No. 9). Her finest works had been taken by French troops as spoils of war from the collections of the Landgrave of Hesse-Cassel. Alexander made another important purchase shortly afterwards from the Dutch banker, W. G. Coesvelt, who had built up an important collection of works by Velázquez, Ribalta, and Zurburán. A few Spanish paintings were also acquired by Nicholas I from Manuel de Godoy, "Prince of Peace," but these did not include any of his Goyas. This artist remained unrepresented in the Hermitage until his portrait of Antonia Zarate was presented by Dr. Armand Hammer in 1972.

During the 1820's and 1830's the Hermitage collections continued to expand; another group of paintings was acquired from Coesvelt, much to the annoyance of Elizabeth Rigby, a visitor to St. Petersburg, who later married Sir Charles Eastlake, President of the Royal Academy and Director of the National Gallery. At the same period more works from the Empress Josephine's collection were sold to Russia by her daughter, the Duchesse de Saint-Leu.

The majority of pictures secured by the Empress Catherine and other collectors of her period were Dutch, Flemish, French and Italian works of the seventeenth or eighteenth centuries. And to this day these schools represent by far the museum's greatest strength. However, under Nicholas I the collection was enriched by a few

paintings of the early Netherlandish school—two works by Jan Van Eyck and two by the Maître de Flémalle—bequeathed by D. P. Tatischev, the High Chamberlain, who had served as Russian Ambassador in Vienna. Further gaps were filled around the middle of the century, when a new taste for earlier schools of painting developed in Russia as it had in western Europe. F. Bruni, the curator of the collection, purchased Flemish primitives, among other items, at the sale of the collection of William III of Holland in 1850. At the same time the tradition of Russian diplomats securing works of art for the Tsar was still maintained. In the same year the Russian Consul-General in Venice, Khvostov, scored a splendid coup by acquiring a number of examples by Titian and other masters of the Venetian *cinquecento* at the sale of the famous Barbarigo collection. Nevertheless, pictures were also weeded out from the Hermitage, and some twelve hundred were disposed of in 1853.

A major development in the history of the Imperial collections occurred in 1852, when a public museum was opened in the Winter Palace and housed in the New Hermitage. This was built by N. Yefimov and V. Stasov to the designs of Leon von Klenze, who had been responsible for the Pinakothek and Glyphthothek in Munich. The New Hermitage is a neo-classical building with an imposing entrance, decorated with ten huge atlantes, carved out of monolithic blocks of Serdobol granite in the workshop of the sculptor Terebenev. The great gallery with the skylight has not changed much since it was opened, and the Dionysus Hall can be easily recognized from K. Ukhtomsky's watercolor of 1853.

An indication of the growing status of the Hermitage collection is the fact that G. F. Waagen, the Director of the Berlin Museum, was commisioned to supervise the preparation of a new inventory and catalogue of the paintings in 1861-62. The catalogue was published in 1863 and served as the basis for later ones.

Meanwhile, substantial additions continued to be made to the Hermitage, among them a superb group of paintings by the German romantic artist, Caspar David Friedrich. In 1861 one particularly active curator, Ghenenov, secured classical vases and frescoes by the school of Raphael from the well-known collection of the Marchese Campana in Rome, and followed this by buying the *Litta Madonna,* attributed to Leonardo da Vinci, in 1866, and Raphael's *Connestabile Madonna* in 1870.

Ghenenov's successor Vasilchikov, was a no less astute buyer: in 1882 he secured Fra Angelico's fresco, *The Virgin and Child with St. Dominic and St. Thomas Aquinas,* which had been painted for the convent of San Domenico in Fiesole. Vasilchikov also persuaded Alexander III to allow the transfer of major pictures from various Imperial residences to the Hermitage.

The steady flow of works into the Hermitage continued with the acquisition of the Galitzine Museum (1886), the Semenov collection of Dutch and Flemish paintings (1910) and Simone Martini's exquisite *Virgin of the Annunciation* from Count Stroganov's collection (1912). Another jewel, Leonardo da Vinci's *"Benois" Madonna,* was secured for the Hermitage in 1914. The representation of the English School—not one of the Hermitage's strengths—was also bolstered in 1916 by the addition of the Khitrovo collection which included Gainsborough's stylish *Portrait of a Lady* (No. 24).

After 1917 the Hermitage was enriched by many items from private collections, such as the Stroganov and Yusupov palaces. It also received the contents of the Academy of Arts, including the Farsetti collection of Italian terracotta *bozzetti* and *modelli,* which had been presented to Paul I, and the Stieglitz Museum, which was rich in examples of the decorative arts. Losses were also sustained when various paintings, prints, drawings, and objects were disposed of at auction or privately, and when a group of old masters was ceded to the Pushkin Museum in Moscow.

One striking feature of Russian art collecting in the years just before the First World War had been the formation of splendid galleries of modern French art by two Moscow merchants, Ivan Morozov and Sergei Shchukin. Subsequently the basis of the Museum of Modern Western Art in Moscow, these collections were redistributed in 1948 between the Hermitage and the Pushkin Museums. Both collectors were gifted with considerable perspicacity. Morozov bought prime examples of the Impressionists and Post-Impressionists, and had a particular admiration for Cézanne and Gauguin; he also arranged for Bonnard and Maurice Denis to undertake decorations for his house. Shchukin, whose taste was more daring, became a patron of Matisse, commissioning him to paint *La Danse* and *La Musique* for the stairwell of his palace and buying a superb group of Picassos. Far from being an isolated phenomenon, their pioneer collecting of modern art should be seen as a logical extension of the aristocratic patronage of the eighteenth century—the patronage of Catherine the Great, Shuvalov, Stroganov, Galitzine, and Yusupov. Thanks to this tradition, the Hermitage presents a magnificent panorama of painting extending from late medieval times to the twentieth century. It also contains vast collections of sculpture and decorative arts of many schools and periods: classical antiquities, medieval and Renaissance treasures, superb tapestries, Russian silver, eighteenth century gold boxes and Sèvres. Nor ought we to forget the astonishing textiles of the fourth to fifth century B.C., which were found in the burial chamber of a tribal chieftain, preserved in ice at Altai.

As the number of tourists who visit Russia and specifically the Hermitage has increased, so has interest in the history of Russian art and architecture. Icons, for instance, have found many new devotees in the West, and Kandinsky and the Constructivists are now hailed as pioneers of the modern movement. However, Russian painting and sculpture of the eighteenth and nineteenth centuries is still not nearly as well known as it deserves. Hence the inclusion in this exhibition of thirteen Russian paintings dating from 1773 to 1906. While no master of international stature emerged during these years, the general level of achievement was very high, as witness the elegant portraits of Levitsky (*e.g.* No. 31)—the subject of Diaghilev's only book—Venetsianov's touching scenes of peasant life (No. 32), and the poetic landscapes (No. 40) of Isaak Levitan—a friend of Chekhov, who used two episodes from the artist's life in *The Seagull.*

Russian patronage during the *ancien régime* was not limited to foreign art but included the native school. The Empress Elizabeth was eager to patronize contemporary Russian artists; and later, Alexander III admired Russian painting. He tried to buy the great collection of *Peredvizhniki* painting formed by the Moscow industrialist, P. M. Tretyakov, but this enterprising Maecenas preferred to found his own museum in Moscow.

On Alexander's death, his son Nicholas II made a major contribution to public knowledge of Russian art by buying one of the finest neo-classical palaces in St. Petersburg, which Rossi had designed for the Grand Duke Mikhail Pavlovich, and turning it into The Russian Museum of the Emperor Alexander III. The former Mikhailovsky Palace (fig. 6) now houses a vast and varied collection of Russian art, including some of the finest works of Briullov (No. 33), whose *Last Days of Pompeii* provided

fig. 6 View of The State Russian Museum, Leningrad.

Bulwer Lytton with the theme for his once famous novel; Ilya Repin (Nos. 38 and 39), who aroused the enthusiasm of Dostoevsky and whose bravura portraits make him the Russian Sargent; Serov (No. 41), a fashionable portrait painter understandably admired by Diaghilev; and Vrubel, whose extravagant mythological scenes in an ornate decorative style that recalls the early work of Kandinsky, are unfortunately too fragile to leave their native country.

The splendor and variety of the Hermitage and the State Russian Museums bear witness to the fact that a love of art is endemic to the Russian character and that Russian art collecting and patronage have consistently been of the highest standard. Inevitably this exhibition includes only a fraction of the two museums' vast holdings, but in their importance and quality these paintings present a cross-section of Russian collecting from the eighteenth century up to 1914 and thus give an idea of the incomparable riches which await the visitor to Leningrad. It is a show that once again emphasizes the fruitful nature of the cultural exchanges that are an agreeable feature of our period.

Abbreviations for Works Frequently Cited

Abbreviation	Publication
Bazin, 1958	Germain Bazin, *Musée de l'Ermitage: les grandes maîtres de la peinture,* Paris, 1958
Benois, 1911	A. Benois, *A Guide to the Picture Gallery of the Hermitage,* St. Petersburg, 1911 (?)
Descargues, 1961	Pierre Descargues, *The Hermitage Museum, Leningrad,* New York, 1961
Hermitage Catalogue, 1958	*Musée de l'Ermitage, départment de l'art occidental, catalogue des peintures,* Moscow, 1958, 2 volumes
Izergina, 1968	A. N. Izergina and the Staff of the State Hermitage, Leningrad, *The Hermitage, Leningrad: French 19th Century Masters,* Prague, 1968
Izergina, *et al.,*1970	A. N. Izergina, A. G. Barskaya and B. A. Zernov, *The Hermitage, Leningrad: 20th Century Masters,* London, 1970
Kuznetsov, 1967	Yu. Kuznetsov, *West European Painting in Museums of the U.S.S.R.* (in Russian), Leningrad, 1967
Kuznetsov, 1972	Yu. Kuznetsov, *The Hermitage Museum: Painting,* Leningrad, 1972
Levinson-Lessing, 1962	W. F. Levinson-Lessing et ses collaborateurs, *l'Ermitage, école flamande et hollandaise,* Prague, 1962
Levinson-Lessing, 1965	W. F. Levinson-Lessing, *The Hermitage, Leningrad: Baroque and Rococo Masters,* London, 1965
Novoselskaya, 1972	I. Novoselskaya and W. F. Levinson-Lessing, *Masterpieces of Painting in the Hermitage Museum,* (U.S.S.R.), 1972
Prokofiev, 1962	V. Prokofiev, *French Painting in U.S.S.R. Museums,* Moscow, 1962
Réau, 1929	Louis Réau, *Catalogue de l'art français dans les musées russes,* Paris, 1929
Somof, 1899	A. Somof, *Ermitage impérial catalogue de la galerie des tableaux, les écoles d'Italie et d'Espagne,* St. Pétersbourg, 1899
Somof, 1901	A. Somof, *Ermitage impérial catalogue de la galerie des tableaux, école néerlandaise ét école allemande,* St. Pétersbourg, 1901
Somof, 1903	A. Somof, *Ermitage impérial catalogue de la galerie des tableaux, école anglaise et école française,* St. Pétersbourg, 1903
Sterling, 1958	Charles Sterling, *Great French Painting in the Hermitage,* New York, 1958
Vsevolozhskaya *et al.,* 1964	S. N. Vsevolozhskaya, I. S. Grigoryeva, and T. D. Fomitcheva, *La Peinture italienne des XIIIe-XVIIIe siècles dans la collection du musée de l'Ermitage,* Hermitage, Leningrad, 1964
Waagen, 1864	G. F. Waagen, *Die Gemäldesammlung in der Kaiserlichen Ermitage zu St. Petersburg,* Munich, 1864
Weiner, 1923	Pierre P. Weiner, *Les Chefs-d'oeuvre de la galerie de tableaux de l'Ermitage à Petrograd,* Munich, 1923 (corrected and revised edition)
Wrangell, 1909	Baron Nicolas Wrangell, *Les Chefs-d'oeuvre de la galerie de tableaux de l'Ermitage impérial à St. Pétersbourg,* London, 1909

Paintings from The State Hermitage Museum

The Editors gratefully acknowledge the valuable contributions to this catalogue made by the following members of The State Hermitage Museum staff:

Italian Painting:
T. Fomicheva
S. Vsevolojskaia

French Painting:
E. Kozhina (seventeenth century)
I. Nemilova (eighteenth century)
A. Barskaia (nineteenth and twentieth centuries)

Spanish Painting:
L. Kagane

Flemish Painting:
M. Varshavskaia

Dutch Painting:
E. Fehner
I. Lennik

German Painting:
N. N. Nikulin

English Painting:
A. E. Krol

Commentaries:
David Lomax	(D.L.)
Constance Lowenthal	(C.L.)
John Richardson	(J.R.)
Edward Sullivan	(E.S.)
Eric Zafran	(E.Z.)

Provenances and Bibliographies:
Elizabeth Dayon
Margaret Duffy
Ann Fernandez
Richard Finnegan
Serena Forbes
Ruth Nicholson
Anne Stone

Translator:
Magdalena Dabrowski

Lucas Cranach the Elder

German: Kronach 1472 — Weimar 1553

1. The Madonna of the Apple Tree *ca.* 1525
Oil on panel transferred to canvas, 34¼ x 23¼ in. (87 x 59 cm.)

Lucas Cranach was a leading German painter of the sixteenth century. He adopted the name of his birthplace, Kronach in Franconia, instead of his family name of Moller. After spending three years working for the Hapsburg Emperor Maximilian I in Vienna, he settled in Wittenberg early in 1505. There he began his lifelong career as court painter to Frederick the Wise, Elector of Saxony, and his successors. Cranach was an early supporter and friend of Martin Luther, and painted many portraits of Luther and other leaders of the Protestant Reformation; however, he also received commissions from Catholics. Cranach was the founder of a large, flourishing workshop, which included two of his sons, Hans and Lucas the Younger, and which produced an enormous number of paintings and prints. Over four hundred paintings survive in all; among the best known are the portraits, hunting scenes, and the famous nude figures of mythological heroines and goddesses. Cranach also painted altarpieces and many smaller devotional pictures for private patrons.

The Madonna of the Apple Tree is signed on the tree trunk with the emblem of the yellow, winged serpent, which was the coat of arms granted to Cranach by the Elector on Three Kings' Day 1508. After the death of his son, Hans, in 1537, Cranach painted this serpent with folded wings, so the Hermitage *Madonna* was certainly executed before this date. It is most likely a product of the 1520's. The facial type of the Virgin, with her wide-set eyes and shapely mouth resembles other faces of women painted by Cranach during these years (*cf. The Magdalen* of 1525, Wallraf-Richartz-Museum, Cologne).

The Madonna is seated in front of a lush German landscape, filled with pine trees. In the distance a fortified cliff towers above a calm lake, a recurrent feature of Cranach's landscapes, which derives from prints by Dürer. Several elements in the painting which appear merely natural have symbolic meanings. The apple tree behind the Virgin symbolizes Eve's temptation of Adam and the fall of mankind from grace. It is Mary, the new Eve, who offers, through her son, a means for mankind to redeem itself from this original sin. Christ's role as Saviour is represented by the piece of bread, which he holds in his hand. This represents the Eucharist, the consecrated bread, that the celebrant receives at Mass.

Cranach painted other half-length Madonnas of similar composition with the Christ Child holding either bread (Bachofen—Burckhardt coll., Basel) or grapes, symbolizing the wine of the Mass (Hermitage).

C.L.

Provenance:
Purchased by Nicholas I in 1851 for
The Hermitage

References:
Waagen, 1864, p. 132, no. 459.
L. Clément de Ris, "Musée impérial de l'Ermitage à Saint-Pétersbourg," *Gazette des Beaux-Arts,* April 1879, p. 350.
W. de Seidlitz, "L'Exposition Cranach à Dresde," *Gazette des Beaux-Arts,* September 1899, p. 197.
Max J. Friedländer, "Die Cranach-Ausstellung in Dresden," *Repertorium für Kunstwissenschaft,* XXII, 1899, p. 243.
Eduard Flechsig, *Cranachstudien,* Leipzig, 1900, pp. 87, 278.
Somof, 1901, no. 459, pp. 55-56.
Ed. Heyck, *Lucas Cranach,* Bielefeld and Leipzig, 1908, no. 37, p. 51 and pp. 67, 74, 76.
Wrangell, 1909, p. 198.
Benois, 1911, p. 441.
Louis Réau, "La Galerie de tableaux de l'Ermitage et la collection Semenov," (deuxième article), *Gazette des Beaux-Arts,* December 1912, p. 475.
Weiner, 1923, p. 261.
Max J. Friedländer and Jakob Rosenberg, *Die Gemälde von Lucas Cranach,* Berlin, 1932, p. 65, no. 187.
Heinrich Lilienfein, *Lukas Cranach und seine Zeit,* Bielefeld and Leipzig, 1944, p. 113, pl. 111.
Gabriel Rouches, *Cranach l'Ancien,* Paris, 1951, pl. 52.
A. Nemiloff, "Lucas Cranach. 400th Anniversary of his Death," (in Russian), *Istkusstvo,* 1953, p. 63.
Bazin, 1958, p. 131, no. 96, and p. 114.
Hermitage Catalogue, 1958, II, no. 684, p. 318, and fig. 306.
A. Nemiloff, "Die Gemälde von Lucas Cranach d.A. in der Staatlichen Ermitage," *Bildende Kunst,* 1959, pp. 176—177.
Descargues, 1961, p. 278.
Kuznetsov, 1967, no. 13.
Kuznetsov, 1972, no. 20.
G. S. Kislych, *Die Bilder von Lucas Cranach d.A. in den Museen der USSR,* Wittenberg, 1973, pp. 81-83.
Werner Schade, *Die Malerfamilie Cranach,* Dresden, 1974, pl. 107, p. 461.

Exhibitions:
Deutsche Kunst-Ausstellung, Cranach-Ausstellung, Dresden, 1899, no. 82.
La Femme et l'artiste de Bellini à Picasso, Bordeaux, 1964, no. 6.
Lucas Cranach, Ausstellung zum seinem 500 Geburtstag, Weimar, 1972, no. 41.

Paolo Caliari called Veronese

Italian: Verona 1528 — Venice 1588

2. Dead Christ with the Virgin Mary and an Angel *ca.* 1580
Oil on canvas, 57¾ x 43⅞ in. (147 x 111.5 cm.)

Veronese received his early training from Antonio Badile, and after a possible visit to Rome, went to Venice in 1553. He was soon commissioned to decorate the ceiling of the Doge's Palace with allegories glorifying the Venetian Republic. His use of rich colors, dramatic action, and inventive compositions filling vast spaces won him immediate success, and he was employed to paint frescoes in numerous villas in the Veneto, as well as portraits of important Venetian citizens. For the churches of Venice he painted several huge canvases depicting festive incidents from the New Testament, with sumptuously dressed figures set amidst grand Palladian buildings. One such work, painted in 1573, led to his being called before the Inquisition on the charge that he had included sacrilegious details. Veronese defended his right to paint directly observed aspects of life, and agreed to change the title from *The Last Supper* to *Feast in the House of Levi* (Accademia, Venice).

During Veronese's later years, his workshop continued to produce large-scale decorative works, but the master himself turned to more somber, religious themes, such as this moving *Dead Christ with the Virgin Mary and an Angel*. It was probably painted for an altar in the Dominican church of *Santi Giovanni e Paolo* in Venice. Both the free style and emotional content are inspired by the late works of Titian (d. 1576). The scene is set in darkness, and nothing detracts from the mood of silent solemnity as the Virgin and angel gaze raptly at the face of Christ. All the wounds of his Passion are revealed to the viewer, and the Crown of Thorns is seen at the lower left. His body rests on a white shroud that covers the Stone of Unction on which it was prepared for burial (John 19: 38-40).

Veronese and his workshop painted many versions of the *Dead Christ* similar to this one (*cf.* examples in a Private coll., Paris; Staatliche Museen, Berlin-Dahlem; Museum of Fine Arts, Boston; Musée des Beaux-Arts, Lille). Some of these are composed in a more symmetrical manner and have another angel on the left side. X-rays reveal that the Hermitage painting also originally included a second angel who clasped Christ's right hand. Veronese painted out this angel and then made small adjustments in the contours of the remaining figures which have become transparent. Thus the painting now appears more heavily weighted to the right side than the artist intended. This painting was engraved by Agostino Carracci in 1582.

C.L.

Provenance:
Church of *Santi Giovanni e Paolo,* Venice
Charles I of England (?)
Duc de Longueville (?)
State Councillor Le Nain (?)
Comte d'Armagnac (?)
Pierre Crozat, Paris, by 1755
The Hermitage, 1772

References:
Marco Boschini, *Le Minere della pittura,* Venice, 1664, pp. 221, 2.
Catalogue des tableaux du cabinet de M. Crozat, Baron de Thiers, Paris, 1755, p. 17.
J. H. Schnitzler, *Notice sur les principaux tableaux du musée impérial de l'Ermitage à St. Pétersbourg,* 1828, p. 35.
Waagen, 1864, p. 71, no. 145.
F. Harck, "Notizen über italienische Bilder in Petersburger Sammlungen," *Repertorium für Kunstwissenschaft,* XIX, 1896, p. 427.
Somof, 1899, no. 145, pp. 32-33.
Benois, 1911, p. 79.
Lionello Venturi, "Saggio sulle opere d'arte italiana a Pietroburgo," *L'Arte,* XV, pp. 210, 212.
Louis Réau, "La Galerie de tableaux de l'Ermitage et la collection Semenov," (premier article), *Gazette des Beaux-Arts,* November 1912, pp. 390, 391.
F. Ingersoll-Smouse, "Les Pièta de Veronese," *Gazette des Beaux-Arts,* January 1926, pp. 23-26.
A. Venturi, *Paolo Veronese (Per Il IV Centenario dalla nascita),* Milan, 1928, pp. 207, 209, p. 208, fig. 145.
R. Pallucchini, *Veronese* (second edition), Bergamo, 1943, p. 43, frontispiece.
P. I. Kostrov, *Restoration and Conservation of the Artistic Monuments, Hermitage, Leningrad,* Moscow, 1955, pp. 41-48, pp. 108-128, pls. 30-52.
Bazin, 1958, p. 64, no. 34, p. 51, notes p. 218.
Hermitage Catalogue, 1958, I, no. 49, p. 74.
Descargues, 1961, pp. 36, 275.
Vsevolozhskaya *et al,* 1964, pp. 239, 240
Franca Zava Boccazzi, *La Basilica dei Santi Giovanni e Paolo in Venezia,* 1965, pp. 326, 327.
Margret Stuffmann, "Les Tableaux de la collection de Pierre Crozat," *Gazette des Beaux-Arts,* July-September, 1968, p. 79, no. 173.
G. Piovene and R. Marini, *L'Opera completa del Veronese,* Milan, 1968, no. 298, pp. 130, 131.
Novoselskaya, 1972, no. 10.
Kuznetsov, 1972, no. 18.
Tamara Fomicieva, "Venetian Painting of the Fifteenth to the Eighteenth Centuries," *Apollo,* December 1974, p. 472, no. 8.

Michelangelo Merisi called Caravaggio

Italian: Caravaggio 1573 — Porto Ercole 1610

3. The Lute Player *ca.* 1596
Oil on canvas, 37 x 46⅞ in. (94 x 119 cm.)

Caravaggio adopted his name from the small Lombard town, where his father worked as a master builder for the local *Marchese*. After his father's death in 1584, Caravaggio was apprenticed for four years to the Milanese painter Simone Peterzano. About 1592-93 he arrived in Rome, where he earned a poor living in various workshops, including for a short time that of Giuseppe Cesari (later the Cavaliere d'Arpino) for whom he supposedly executed still life compositions of flowers and fruits. Not until about 1596, when he was introduced to the influential Cardinal del Monte, did Caravaggio begin to gain recognition. For the Cardinal and his circle, Caravaggio probably painted both his series of effete youths and his genre scenes of card players and fortune tellers.

It was apparently Cardinal del Monte who secured for Caravaggio his first major religious commission, the two lateral paintings in the Contarelli Chapel of *San Luigi dei Francesi* representing *The Calling* and *Martyrdom of St. Matthew*. From this time on Caravaggio received a steady stream of commissions for his powerful religious works. Influenced by the new Counter-Reformation beliefs of such men as St. Filipo Neri, these works sought to involve the spectator directly in the action, and made dramatic use of light, while employing ordinary individuals in natural poses.

Caravaggio's revolutionary approach was not appreciated by all members of the clergy, and his *Death of the Virgin* (Louvre, Paris), for example, was rejected as sacrilegious by the fathers of *Santa Maria della Scala* in 1606, only to be purchased at a high price by the Duke of Mantua on the recommendation of Rubens.

As a culmination to a series of violent incidents, Caravaggio quarreled with and killed a tennis opponent and had to flee from Rome in late May of 1606. For the remainder of his life, he wandered throughout southern Italy, Malta, and Sicily executing a series of somber, large-scale religious works. Just as a papal pardon was imminent, Caravaggio, on his way from Naples to Rome, died of a malignant fever, on July 18, 1610.

Caravaggio's art had an immense impact throughout Europe. Every major later seventeenth century master from Rubens to Rembrandt and Vermeer to Velázquez was in some degree influenced by his innovations. In addition he had many imitators in France, Holland, and Spain, as well as Italy, who adopted his subjects and effects, but none could rival the breadth of Caravaggio's unique, if often disturbing, imagination or his consummate skill.

In his biography of Caravaggio the Roman painter Giovanni Baglione (1642) describing works done by Caravaggio for Cardinal del Monte writes, "He also made a painting of a youth playing a lute which was so lifelike and realistic in appearance, with a vase of flowers filled with water in which one can easily distinguish the reflections of a window and other objects in the room, and on the flowers is fresh dew which is rendered with exquisite

Provenance:
Cardinal del Monte, Rome, *ca.* 1596
Giustiniani Collection, Rome by *ca.* 1640
 from which it was purchased in 1808 through
 Baron Vivant Denon by
The Hermitage

References:
Giovanni Baglione, *Le Vite de'pittori scultori et architetti,* Rome, 1642, p. 136.
G. P. Bellori, *Vite de' pittori, scultori et architetti,* Rome, 1672, p. 204.
Joanne M. Silos, *Pinacotheca romana,* Rome, 1673, pp. 90-91.
Friedrich Wilhelm von Ramdohr, *Ueber Mahlerei und Bildhauerarbeit in Rom,* III, Leipzig, 1787, p. 41.
A. Paillet and H. Delaroche, *Catalogue historique et raisonné de tableaux . . . du Prince Giustiniani, Paris,* 1812, pp. 85-86, no. 89.
Louis Viardot, *Les Musées d'Allemagne et de Russie,* Paris, 1814, p. 472.
Waagen, 1864, p. 82, no. 217.
Somof, 1899, p. 12, no. 217.
Wolfgang Kallab, "Caravaggio," *Jahrbuch der kunsthistorischen Sammlungen des allerhöchsten Kaiserhauses,* 1906-1907, p. 280, fig. 4.
Lionello Venturi, "Studii su Michelangelo da Caravaggio," *L'Arte,* 1910, pp. 197-198.
Benois, 1911, p. 97.
Matteo Marangoni, "Valori mal noti e trascurati della pittura italiana . . . ," *Rivista d'arte,* 1917-1918, p. 13.
Matteo Marangoni, *Il Caravaggio,* Venice, 1922, pp. 14, 22, pl. V.
Matteo Marangoni, "Quattro Caravaggio Smarriti," *Dedalo,* February 1922, pp. 783-784, 789.
Hermann Voss, "Caravaggios Frühzeit," *Jahrbuch der preussischen Kunstsammlungen,* 1923, pp. 79-80.
Weiner, 1923, p. 59.
Ernst Benkard, *Caravaggio-Studien,* Berlin, 1928, pp. 113-124, pl. 21.
Nikolaus Pevsner, *Barockmalerei in den romanischen Ländern,* Potsdam, 1928, I, pp. 126-127.
Leopold Zahn, *Caravaggio,* Berlin, 1928, pp .11-12, 34-35, pl. V.
Ludwig Schüdt, *Caravaggio,* Vienna, 1942, pp. 9, 44 (no. 9), pl. 9.
Denis Mahon, *"Egregius in Urbe Pictor:* Caravaggio Revised," *The Burlington Magazine,* July 1951, p. 233.
Mario Valsecchi, *Caravaggio,* second edition, Milan-Florence, 1951, fig. 26.
Lionello Venturi, *Il Caravaggio,* Novara, 1951, pp. 8, 15, 49, pl. 11.

accuracy. And this he said was the most beautiful painting he ever made." This is undoubtedly the painting now in the Hermitage.

The Lute Player is one of a group of paintings, including *Bacchus,* (Uffizi, Florence), *Boy Bitten by a Lizard* (Longhi coll., Florence), and *The Musicians* (Metropolitan Museum of Art, New York, fig. 7) from Caravaggio's Roman period of the 1590's, which depict semi-nude, androgynous youths with flowers, fruits, and musical instruments. These unusual works have been interpreted as both allegories of love and a variety of *vanitas.* The figure in *The Lute Player* has even mistakenly been called a girl. The key to understanding the ambiguous nature of this group is to be found in the personalities of Caravaggio and his patron, Cardinal del Monte. The latter, as Francis Haskell (1963) has written, "lived largely for pleasure—banquets, theatrical entertainment, parties 'where as there were no ladies present the dancing was done by boys dressed as girls,' and this side of his life has been reflected in a series of canvases of effeminate boys by Caravaggio." Donald Posner (1971) has further analyzed the "homo-erotic content" of these paintings, remarking that "Caravaggio's youths do not merely address themselves to the spectator—they solicit him."

In the Hermitage painting the charms of the youth are complemented by a display of flowers and fruit that certainly justifies the stories about Caravaggio's early training as a specialist in such still lifes. However, this also helps, as Posner observed, "to heighten the sensuous appeal of the representation . . . with the tempting suggestion of fragrant aromas and delicious flavors . . . and [was] chosen to serve as a gloss on the sensuous theme of the picture"

Even more important to an understanding of the painting is the connection made between music and love. Caravaggio several times, as in *The Flight to Egypt* (Galleria Doria-Pamphili, Rome) and the *Amor Victorious* (Staatliche Museen, Berlin-Dahlem), included realistic musical scores, offering the viewer a suggestion of aural accompaniment to his visual experience. In *The Lute Player* and the Metropolitan Museum's *The Musicians,* however, the scores and the instruments are symbolic. While in the latter painting the music has not yet begun and the lutenist is still tuning his instrument, both works, in Professor Posner's words, "share one striking detail, a violin and a bow at the front edge of the picture. The neck of the violin faces outward, toward the spectator . . . The point is plain . . . the lutenist invites the spectator to take up the violin and join him in making 'beautiful music.' " Even the music itself conveys this intention in the Hermitage painting, for the words written in the partbook, from which the lutenist sings, read *Voi sapete ch'* and have been identified (see Bazin, 1958) as being the beginning of the madrigal *Voi sapete ch'io v'amo* by the sixteenth century Franco-Flemish composer Jacques Arcadelt. On the cover of the other partbook which, like the violin, projects toward the viewer is written *Bassus* (*i.e.* the bass part), and this too may be part of the same conceit.

The features of the lute player in the Hermitage painting and his

Fritz Baumgart, "Die Anfänge Caravaggios," *Zeitschrift für Kunstwissenschaft,* 1952, pp. 95-97, fig. 6.

Roberto Longhi, *Il Caravaggio,* Milan, 1952 pp. 11, 15, 18, 19.

Denis Mahon, "Addenda to Caravaggio," *The Burlington Magazine,* January 1952, pp. 4, 7, 8, 11, fig. 6.

Bernard Berenson, *Caravaggio,* London, 1953, pp. 8, 61, pl. 10.

Roger Hinks, *Michelangelo Merisi da Cara-vaggio,* New York, 1953, p. 50-51, 98, pl. 11.

Denis Mahon, "On Some Aspects of Caravaggio and His Times," *The Metropolitan Museum of Art Bulletin,* October 1953, pp. 37, 43, 44.

Stella Mary Pearce, "Costume in Caravaggio's Painting," *Magazine of Art,* January 1953, p. 154.

Agnes Czobor, "Autoritratti del giovane Caravaggio," *Acta Historiae Artium Academiae Scientiarum Hungaricae,* 1954, pp. 204, 206, 208, 209, 210, fig. 8.

Hanns Swarzenski, "Carvaggio and Still-Life Painting, Notes on a Recent Acquisition," *Bulletin of the Museum of Fine Arts Boston,* 1954, pp. 28-29, 31, 32, fig. 7.

Fritz Baumgart, *Caravaggio, Kunst und Wirk-lichkeit,* Berlin, 1955, pp. 18-19, 95.

Walter Friedländer, *Caravaggio Studies,* Princeton, 1955, *passim.*

Leningrad, Hermitage: Italian Art, 14th-18th Centuries, Moscow, 1955, p. 50.

T. P. Znamerovskaya, *Michelangelo da Cara-vaggio,* Moscow, 1955, p. 29.

Kurt Bauch, "Zur Ikonographie von Caravaggios Frühwerken," *Kunstgeschichtliche Studien für Hans Kauffmann,* Berlin, 1956, pp. 254, 256.

Sergio Samek Ludovici, *Vita del Caravaggio dalle testimonianze del suo tempo,* Milan, 1956, pp. 44, 56, 97, 119.

Hermitage Catalogue, 1958, I, pp. 102-103, no. 45, fig. 46.

Hugo Wagner, *Michelangelo da Caravaggio,* Bern, 1958, pp. 20-21.

Berne Joffroy, *Le Dossier Caravage,* Paris, 1959, *passim.*

Luigi Salerno, "The Picture Gallery of Vincenzo Giustiniani, III, The Inventory, Part II," *The Burlington Magazine,* April 1960, p. 135, no. 8.

Descargues, 1961, pp. 106-107.

René Jullian, *Caravage,* Lyon-Paris, 1961, pp. 46-47, 49, 226, pl. III.

Costantino Baroni, *All the Paintings of Caravaggio,* New York, 1962, p. 19, pl. 8.

Silvino Borla, "1593: Arrivo del Caravaggio a Roma," *Emporium,* January 1962, p. 16.

Giuseppe de Logu, *Caravaggio,* Milan, 1962, pp. 9, 30, 31, 140, fig. 4.

Silvino Borla, "Opere milanesi del Caravaggio," *Emporium,* October 1963, pp. 157-162.

Detail of No. 3

counterpart in *The Musicians* are almost identical, and it is possible that they represent an actual youth in Cardinal del Monte's employ, but they are certainly not, as has sometimes been stated, self-portraits of the young Caravaggio.

The sensuous appeal of *The Lute Player* is matched by the artist's equally sensuous technique, and his brilliant, if idiosyncratic rendering of light. One source of light illuminates the boy's body, the fruit, and flowers, endowing them all with a full, physical presence. But the lute player's face catches the light in such a way that it seems stylized and artificial. The dark background plane which sets off the figure is animated by a triangular band of light crossing it at the upper right. This also occurs in Caravaggio's *Penitent Magdalen* (Galleria Doria-Pamphili, Rome). Yet another source of light is indicated, as was observed by Baglione, in the reflected window seen on the vase, a device repeated in the *Boy Bitten by a Lizard*.

A copy of *The Lute Player* attributed to Carlo Saraceni (Galleria Barberini, Rome) eliminates the flowers and fruit and replaces the violin with a flute. Caravaggio's paintings of musicians inspired other later Italian painters such as Gentileschi and Manfredi, but their works are almost totally devoid of the erotic qualities with which Caravaggio invested his originals.

E.Z.

fig. 7. Caravaggio, *The Musicians, ca.* 1596, The Metropolitan Museum of Art, New York, Rogers Fund, 1952.

Francis Haskell, *Patrons and Painters,* New York, 1963, pp. 28-29.

Vsevolozhskaya, *et al.,* 1964, pp. 257-258, 301, 307, fig. 122, 123.

René Jullian, "Un Peintre et son marchand à Rome vers la fin du XVIᵉ siècle," *Pour Daniel-Henry Kahnweiler,* New York, 1965, pp. 138-143.

Luigi Salerno *et al.,* "Poesia e simboli nel Caravaggio," *Palatino,* April-June 1966, p. 112.

Y. Kuznetsov, *West European Still-Life Painting,* Leningrad-Moscow, 1966, pp. 196-197, (Russian).

Michael Kitson, *The Complete Paintings of Caravaggio,* New York, 1967, p. 87, no. 13.

Kuznetsov, 1967, no. 23.

Roberto Longhi, *"Me Pinxit e quesiti caravaggeschi 1928-1934,"* Edizone delle opere complete di Roberto Longhi, IV, Florence, 1968, pp. 90, 120, pl. 165.

Christoph L. Frommel, "Caravaggio und seine Modelle," *Castrum Peregrini,* 96, 1970, pp. 31, 39, fig. b.

S. N. Vsevolozhskaya, *Paintings by Caravaggio and His School in the Collections of the Hermitage,* Leningrad, 1970, pp. 9-18.

Maurizio Calvesi, "Caravaggio o la ricerca della salvazione," *Storia dell'arte,* 9-10, 1971, pp. 110, 111, 141.

Gian Alberto dell'Acqua and Mia Cinotti, *Il Caravaggio e le sue grandi opere da San Luigi dei Francesi,* Milan, 1971, pp. 17, 18, 93-94, 182 (notes 161-163), fig. 7.

Christoph L. Frommel, "Caravaggios Frühwerk und der Kardinal Francesco Maria del Monte," *Storia dell'arte,* 9-10, 1971, *passim.*

W. Chandler Kirwin, "Addendum to Cardinal Francesco Maria del Monte's Inventory." *Storia dell'arte,* 9-10, 1971, p. 55.

Donald Posner, "Caravaggio's Homo-Erotic Early Works," *The Art Quarterly,* Autumn, 1971, pp. 301, 303-304, 307, 313, 318, fig. 4.

Richard Spear, *Caravaggio and His Followers,* Cleveland, 1971, p. 3.

Luigi Spezzeferro, "La Cultura del Cardinal del Monte e il primo tempo del Caravaggio," *Storia dell'arte,* 9-10, 1971, pp. 57, 84, 85-86, 88-89.

Kuznetsov, 1972, no. 24.

Mia Cinotti *et al., Immagine del Caravaggio,* Bergamo, 1973, p. 64, no. 7, pl. 7.

Valerio Mariani, *Caravaggio,* Rome, 1973, p. 40, pl. 11.

"Editorial: Treasures of the North," *Apollo,* December 1974, p. 441.

Arturo Bovi, *Caravaggio,* Florence, 1974, pp. 150-153.

Exhibitions:

Caravaggio and His Followers, The Hermitage, Leningrad, 1973, no. 18.

Detail of No. 3

Domenico Fetti

Italian: Rome 1588/9 — Venice 1623

4. Portrait of an Actor *ca.* 1621-23
Oil on canvas, 41⅛ x 31¾ in. (104.5 x 80.5 cm.)

As a youth Fetti studied with the Florentine trained painter Cigoli but was also influenced by Caravaggio and Elsheimer. In 1613 he was appointed court painter by the new Duke of Mantua, Ferdinando II Gonzaga. In Mantua Fetti not only saw works by Rubens, but also discovered the paintings of the Venetian masters, Titian, Tintoretto, and Bassano, whose rich and atmospheric style he soon adopted. Although he painted some large-scale frescoes, Fetti's true forte was small cabinet pictures, particularly an inventive series illustrating the parables of the New Testament.

In 1621 the Duke sent Fetti to Venice to purchase new works of art, and he returned there in the fall of 1622, remaining until his death. Fetti, along with the German-born artist Johann Lys, can be credited with revitalizing the Venetian school of painting. His refined *tenebroso* manner inspired such later painters active in Venice as Strozzi, Maffei, and Mazzoni.

The few known portraits by Fetti are noteworthy both for their painterliness and straightforward humanity, which probably derived from his familiarity with portraits by Rubens and Van Dyck. In the nineteenth century this impressive portrait in the Hermitage was mistakenly identified as the Mantuan actor Giovanni Gabrielli on the evidence of an engraving by Agostino Carracci to which it bears little resemblance. Giuseppe de Logu (1967) proposed that it and another version in the Accademia, Venice, represent the composer Claudio Monteverdi. However, the comparison offered between the paintings and the only certain engraved portrait of Monteverdi is far from convincing.

A more likely solution suggested by Pamela Askew (1954) is that this portrait, the one in Venice, and a bust-length version in Manchester represent the Mantuan-born actor Tristano Martinelli (1555-1630), who was the leading comedian of his time. He was in Mantua from 1614 until 1620 and again from mid-1621 until his departure for Venice in 1623, so that Fetti could easily have painted his portrait. The years 1621-23, when Martinelli was in his mid-sixties, seem the most likely time for this. In the Le Moyne sale of 1912, a bust-length pastel after Fetti's portrait attributed to Fragonard was entitled *Portrait de l'auteur et acteur Martinelli,* thus further supporting this identification.

There seems no reason to regard the harlequin's mask as symbolic. Fetti, as revealed by the dedication of a Venetian comedy to him in 1619, had connections with the theater; and if the man is Martinelli, the mask is quite simply the chief tool of his trade. Its bizarre, frozen appearance, with huge, empty eye holes, contrasts with the mobile, touchingly human·features of the man, whose penetrating, red-rimmed eyes are fixed upon the viewer. His isolation within the heavily shadowed, indistinct space creates an air of mystery and nobility.

E.Z.

Provenance:
Cardinal Mazarin Collection, Paris by 1653
Pierre Crozat Collection, Paris by 1755
The Hermitage, 1772

References:
Catalogue des Tableaux du cabinet de M. Crozat, Paris, 1755, p. 29.
J. P. Mariette, *Recueil d'estampes,* Paris, 1763, II, p. 8, no. CIX.
Inventaire de tous les meubles du Cardinal Mazarin, dressé en 1653, London, 1861, p. 367.
Waagen, 1864, p. 85, no. 236.
Gabriel-Jules, Comte de Cosnac, *Les Richesses du Palais Mazarin,* Paris, 1884, p. 342, no. 1266.
Somof, 1899, pp. 53-54, no. 236.
Catalogues de Ventes et Livrets de Salons, Paris, 1909, p. 29, no. 114.
Benois, 1911, p. 103.
R. Oldenbourg, *Domenico Fetti,* Rome, 1921, p. 13.
Thomas Bodkin "Domenico Fetti," *Studies, An Irish Quarterly Review,* 1923, pp. 606-7.
Weiner, 1923, pl. 64.
Gino Fogolari, in *Il Ritratto italiano dal Caravaggio al Tiepolo,* U. Ojetti (ed.), Bergamo, 1927, pp. 107-8, 120.
Giuseppe Fiocco, *Venetian Painting of the Seicento and the Settecento,* New York, 1929, p. 17, pl. 17.
Frank Jewett Mather, *Venetian Painters,* New York, 1936, p. 432, fig. 114.
Denis Mahon, *Studies in Seicento Art and Theory,* London, 1947, p. 267, fig. 50.
Pamela Askew, *Domenico Fetti,* dissertation, Courtauld Institute, 1954.
Bazin, 1958, p. 73, pl. 49.
Hermitage Catalogue, 1958, I, p. 202, no. 153.
Descargues, 1961, pp. 36, 276.
St. John Gore, *Primitives to Picasso,* Royal Academy of Arts, London, 1962, p. 53.
Vsevolozhskaya, *et al.,* 1964, p. 261, nos. 129, 130, pp. 302, 310.
Levinson-Lessing, 1965, pl. 9.
Giuseppe de Logu, "An Unknown Portrait of Monteverdi by Domenico Feti," *The Burlington Magazine,* December 1967, pp. 706-709.
Venetian Baroque and Rococo, Ferens Art Gallery, Kingston-upon-Hull, England, 1967, p. 19, no. 20.
Margaret Stuffman, "Les Tableaux de la Collection de Pierre Crozat," *Gazette des Beaux-Arts,* July-September 1968, p. 68, no. 92.
Barbara Scott, "Pierre Crozat," *Apollo,* January 1973, p. 17, fig. 11, p. 18.

Exhibitions:
Exhibition of Portraits, The Hermitage, Leningrad, 1938, no. 184.

Francesco Guardi

Italian: Venice 1712 — Venice 1793

5. Landscape *ca.* 1775-85
Oil on canvas, 46⅞ x 60 in. (119 x 152.5 cm.)
Signed lower right: *Fran.co de Guardj F.*

Little is known about the life and career of Francesco Guardi. He was trained in the studio of his elder brother, Gianantonio (1699-1760), but the extent of their collaboration and the date at which Francesco became interested in *vedute* (view painting) remain unclear. Certainly Francesco's individuality does not emerge until after the death of his brother, when he largely abandoned figure painting for *vedute*.

He seems to have been employed mainly by Englishmen living in Venice, such as the picture-restorer, Peter Edwards, and the British Resident, John Strange. In 1766 and 1782 Guardi was commissioned to record ceremonies arranged for the visits of important dignitaries to the city.

Guardi aroused little interest among his Venetian contemporaries, who probably regarded him as only a follower of the more famous Canaletto. It was not until 1784 that he was elected to the Academy of Fine Arts as a *pittore prospettico.* An extremely prolific artist, he remained active until his death in 1793, only four years before the proclamation of the end of the Republic by Napoleon.

The major stylistic influences on Guardi's early landscapes and view paintings were Marco Ricci and Canaletto, with whom he may have studied. However, he soon turned away from the latter's meticulous technique and airless rendering of Venetian light. Instead Guardi sought to capture the shimmering atmosphere of the city, in which straight lines dissolve and solid forms seem to float between sky and water. This fascination with atmospheric effects combined with his disregard for topographical accuracy was most brilliantly exploited in his *capricci,* scenes of imaginary, often ruined buildings, with a few sketchily drawn figures by the edge of a lagoon. Guardi's sensitive rendering of light flickering upon buildings and water and his nervous brushwork create an impression of transience that perfectly expresses the character of Venice.

The Hermitage painting is one of a small group of rural landscapes by Guardi in which earth, trees, and vegetation rather than water and architecture are the dominant elements. It is typical of Guardi's rather dark later style, in which strong tonal contrasts are created by placing bright, sunlit areas next to deeply shadowed ones. The small, summarily drawn figures, the jagged rocks and the towering trees twisted into sinuous patterns create a mood of picturesque unrest which is reminiscent of the landscapes of Magnasco.

D.L.

Provenance:
Gatchina Palace (near St. Petersburg)
The Hermitage, 1928

References:
Victor Lasareff, "Francesco and Gianantonio Guardi," *The Burlington Magazine,* August 1934, p. 71, pl. IV-A.
Max Goering, *Francesco Guardi,* Vienna, 1944, pp. 32, 72, note 24.
Hermitage Catalogue, 1958, I, no. 4305, p. 82, fig. 28, p. 81.
Descargues, 1961, p. 71.
Vsevolozhskaya, *et. al.,* 1964, pp. 287, 288, 306, and pl. 190.
Levinson-Lessing, 1965, no. 27.
Rodolfo Pallucchini, "Note sulla mostra dei Guardi," *Arte Veneta,* 1965, p. 228.
Edoardo Arslan, "Considerazioni sul vedutismo di Francesco Guardi," *Problemi Guardeschi,* Venice, 1967, p. 9.
Antonio Morassi, "The 'Lagoonscapes' of Francesco Guardi," *Apollo,* July, 1969, p. 44.
Antonio Morassi, *Antonio e Francesco Guardi,* Venice, 1973, I, p. 281; and II, no. 998 figs. 880, 881, 910.
Luigina Bortolatto, *L'Opera completa di Francesco Guardi,* Milan, 1974, no. 610.

Exhibitions:
Mostra dei Guardi, Venice, Palazzo Grassi, 1965. no. 61.

Giovanni Battista Tiepolo

Italian: Venice 1696 — Madrid 1770

6. Maecenas Presenting the Arts to Augustus *ca.* 1743
Oil on canvas, 27⅜ x 35¼ in. (69.6 x 89.7 cm.)

Tiepolo received his first training from the Venetian painter Lazzarini, but his earliest paintings of about 1715-16 reveal a debt to the dark, dramatic style of Piazzetta (1683-1754). Probably under the influence of works by Sebastiano Ricci (1659-1734), who had returned to Venice in 1717, he soon began to lighten his palette and eliminate strong contrasts of light and shadow. Tiepolo owed much to Ricci who was one of the first artists to abandon a dark seventeenth century style and employ bright colors and light tonalities reminiscent of the sixteenth century Venetian master, Paolo Veronese. However, Tiepolo's technical virtuosity and power of invention soon surpassed that of Ricci.

By the middle of the 1720's, Tiepolo had developed a brilliant style of his own perfectly suited to the large fresco decorations which he was called upon to execute in Venice and throughout northern Italy. By the 1730's he was not only the leading Venetian painter, but an artist of European fame. In 1750, accompanied by his sons Domenico and Lorenzo, he went to Würzburg in Germany to paint the frescoes in the palace of the Prince-Bishop. Probably the greatest achievement of his career, these show Tiepolo's extraordinary capacity for organizing numerous figures and other elements on ceilings in such a way that they are perfectly co-ordinated with the surrounding architecture. After his return to Venice in 1753, he remained constantly at work on frescoes, altarpieces, and easel paintings which were usually preceded by countless drawings and sketches. In 1762, summoned by Charles III, Tiepolo went to Spain to paint frescoes in the Royal Palace in Madrid, and died there in 1770.

Maecenas Presenting the Arts to Augustus is one of two paintings commissioned from Tiepolo in 1743 by the Venetian writer and art connoisseur, Francesco Algarotti for Count Brühl, the powerful minister and artistic advisor of Augustus III, Elector of Saxony and King of Poland. In the hope that Brühl would intercede with the King to grant him the title of superintendent of the Royal buildings and collections in Dresden, Algarotti was careful to choose subjects that would flatter this influential minister.

Algarotti's intention, clearly expressed in his letters, was to suggest in this work that Brühl was a modern Maecenas whose artistic judgment had made the court of the new Augustus a flourishing artistic center. The palace seen in the right background is that built by Brühl in Dresden on the banks of the Elbe.

Maecenas, who died in 8 B.C., was the friend and counselor of the Emperor Augustus. In the Hermitage picture, he is shown standing at the left near Augustus who is seated on his throne between statues of Apollo and Athena. Maecenas gestures toward the personifications of the arts who stand or kneel before the Emperor. In the foreground appears "Painting" with her palette and brushes, then "Sculpture" who rests her hand on a bust, and next to her the less prominent figure of "Architecture," indicated by a compass.

Provenance:
Commissioned by Francesco Algarotti 1743
Count Brühl, Dresden by 1744
Purchased from Brühl's estate
  by Catherine II in 1769
Gatchina Palace (near St. Petersburg)
The Hermitage, 1882

References:
Somof, 1899, p. 126, no. 1671.
Wrangell, 1909, p. 38.
E. de Liphart, "Acquisitions of The Imperial Hermitage" *Starye Gody,* January 1910, p.13.
Eduard Sack, *Giambattista und Domenico Tiepolo: Ihr Leben und ihre Werke,* Hamburg, 1910, p. 118, p. 206, no. 423, fig. 204.
Pompeo Molmenti, *Tiepolo, La vie et l'oeuvre du peintre,* Paris, 1911, pp. 215, 216, pl. 230.
Gino Fogolari, "L'Accademia veneziana di pittura e scoltura del settecento," *L'Arte,* July-August 1913, p. 255.
Weiner, 1923, p. 70.
Hans Posse, "Die Briefe des Grafen Francesco Algarotti an den sächsischen Hof und seine Bilderkäufe für die Dresdner Gemäldegalerie 1743-1747," *Jahrbuch der preussischen Kunstsammlungen,* 1931, *Beiheft,* p. 49 note 2.
Michael Levey, "Tiepolo's 'Empire of Flora'," *The Burlington Magazine,* March 1957, p. 89.
Bazin, 1958, fig. 55, pp. 82 and 223, note 120.
Hermitage Catalogue, 1958, I, no. 4, p. 200, fig. 123.
Michael Levey, "Two Paintings by Tiepolo from the Algarotti Collection," *The Burlington Magazine,* September, 1960, p. 250.
Descargues, 1961, pp. 65, 108.
Antonio Morassi, *A Complete Catalogue of the Paintings of G. B. Tiepolo,* Greenwich, Conn., 1962, p. 15; fig. 312.
Francis Haskell, *Patrons and Painters,* New York, 1963, pp. 353, 354.
Vsevolozhskaya, *et al.,* 1964, pp. 281, 303, pls. 174, 175.
Levinson-Lessing, 1965, no. 22.
Kuznetsov, 1967, no. 72.
Guido Piovene and Anna Pallucchini, *L'Opera completa di Giambattista Tiepolo,* Milan, 1968, no. 153.
Kuznetsov, 1972, no. 30.
Novoselskaya, 1972, no. 34.
Fern Rusk Shapley, *Paintings from the Samuel H. Kress Collection: Italian Schools XVI-XVIII Century,* London, 1973, p. 145.
Tamara Fomicieva, "Ventian Painting of the Fifteenth to Eighteenth Centuries," *Apollo,* December 1974, p. 477.

Behind the three women stands the blind Homer who represents "Poetry." The expression of displeasure on the face of Augustus, which hardly seems appropriate in this context, is perhaps a reference to the Emperor's bad temper which, according to the Roman writer Cassius Dio, only Maecenas was adept at soothing.

Instead of reconstructing a Roman palace, Tiepolo has characteristically placed the scene in an airy and spacious setting inspired by the architectural backgrounds often found in Veronese's paintings. Tiepolo's debt to Veronese is also apparent in the richly brocaded dress of the woman in the foreground, the silhouetting of the colonnade against a blue sky, and the stage-like space in which the figures perform their roles. The Hermitage painting is a superb example of Tiepolo's ability to infuse a potentially pompous allegory with an air of lively theatricality and fantasy.

The pendant to *Maecenas* is the *Realm of Flora* (The Fine Arts Museums of San Francisco, fig. 8). This also contains an allusion to Brühl in the form of a fountain which embellished another of his Dresden houses. Algarotti intended this allegory to show how Brühl's partonage of the arts, like the rule of the goddess of spring, could transform *"les lieux plus sauvages"* into *"endroits délicieux."* Despite Tiepolo's marvelous pair of paintings, Algarotti's effort was unsuccessful, for he did not receive the position which he desired.

D.L.

fig. 8. G. B. Tiepolo, *The Realm of Flora*, ca. 1743, Kress Collection, The Fine Arts Museums of San Francisco.

Detail of No. 6

Nicolas Poussin

French: Les Andelys 1594 — Rome 1665

7. Tancred and Erminia *ca.* 1631
Oil on canvas, 38¾ x 57¾ in. (98.5 x 146.8 cm.)

Poussin was both the greatest French painter of the seventeenth century and the first French artist to enjoy European fame. Although virtually his whole career was spent in Rome, the influence of his work and ideas was of decisive importance for the development of French painting over the next two centuries, appealing to artists as diverse as David and Delacroix, Cézanne and Seurat. During his early years in Rome, he experimented with the styles of such masters as Giovanni Lanfranco and Andrea Sacchi. But by the mid-1630's he had developed a "classical" style which reflected his study of ancient art and such masters of the sixteenth and early seventeenth centuries as Raphael, Annibale Carracci and Domenichino.

Poussin's conviction that art must serve a moral and didactic purpose and not simply please the eye, led him to evolve a severe style which demanded that the varied actions and expressions of each figure be carefully studied by the viewer. His art always conveys his seriousness of purpose and reveals his brilliant capacity for extracting the essence of a story.

Born in Normandy, where he received little formal artistic education, Poussin went to Paris, probably in 1612. In 1624 he arrived in Rome, the leading art center in Europe. His first years were difficult, but in 1628 he received recognition when he was given the commission for an altarpiece in St. Peter's. He soon, however, abandoned such monumental painting to devote himself to smaller pictures of religious, historical and mythological themes, done primarily for French collectors. By the end of the 1630's Poussin was so celebrated that Cardinal Richelieu insisted he return to Paris to work for Louis XIII. Soon after his arrival at court in 1640, he was named *peintre du roi* and charged with many commissions, including decorations for the *Grande Galerie* of the Louvre. Temperamentally unsuited to such tasks and disgusted by the intrigues of envious rivals, he departed for Rome in 1642, never to return again to France. In Rome he worked almost exclusively for his cultivated French patrons, remaining aloof from the Roman art community. Poussin's later paintings became ever richer and more profound in content achieving through their austere formal language a unique fusion of classical and Christian elements.

Tancred and Erminia depicts an episode from Torquato Tasso's epic poem, *Gerusalemme Liberata*. Book XIX of this famous sixteenth century work concerning the capture of Jerusalem during the First Crusade, relates how Erminia, Princess of Antioch, found her beloved Tancred, one of the crusader knights, lying wounded after he had killed the infidel warrior, Argantes. With the help of Vafrino, Tancred's squire, she successfully revived her lover and cut off her own hair to bind his wounds.

Poussin has depicted the moment when Erminia overcomes her grief, and cuts her hair. Her use of Tancred's sword for this purpose is Poussin's own invention. Her face has an intentness that mirrors her stoic resolve in contrast to the passive solicitude of Vafrino who supports the limp body of Tancred.

Provenance:
Jacques-André-Joseph Aved, Paris, by 1766
Purchased for Catherine II at the Aved Sale,
 Paris, November 24, 1766
The Hermitage

References:
*Catalogue raisonné de tableaux...qui composent
 le cabinet du feu M. Aved,* Rémy, Paris,
 November 24, 1766, no. 106.
J. H. Schnitzler, *Notice sur les principaux
 tableaux du musée impérial de l'Ermitage à
 St. Pétersbourg,* 1828, pp. 67, 68.
John Smith, *A Catalogue Raisonné of the Works
 of the Most Eminent Dutch, Flemish and
 French Painters,* London, 1837, VIII, pp. 147,
 148, no. 290.
Paul Lacroix, "Musée du palais de l'Ermitage
 sous le règne de Catherine II," (reprint of 1774
 Hermitage catalogue), *Revue Universelle des
 Arts,* April-September 1861, p. 165, no. 11.
A. Andreson, *Nicolas Poussin, Verzeichniss der
 nach seinem Gemälden gefertigen Kup-
 ferstiche,* Leipzig, 1863, no. 414.
Waagen, 1864, p. 284, no. 1408.
L. Dussieux, *Les Artistes français à l'étranger,*
 Paris and Lyon, 1876, p. 579.
Somof, 1903, no. 1408, pp. 78, 79.
A. Benois, 1911, p. 149.
Louis Réau, "La Galerie de tableaux de
 l'Ermitage et la collection Semenov,"
 (premier article), *Gazette des Beaux-Arts,*
 November 1912, p. 394.
Otto Grautoff, *Nicolas Poussin,* Munich, 1914,
 I, pp. 108, 109, II. no. 39.
Emile Magne, *Nicolas Poussin, premier peintre
 du roi, 1594-1665,* Paris and Brussels, 1914,
 p. 219, no. 339.
Réau, 1929, no. 292.
Louis Hourticq, *La Jeunesse de Poussin,* Paris,
 1937, pp. 84, 98ff, fig. XVI.
Maurice Denis, "Poussin et notre temps,"
 L'Amour de l'Art, June 1938, facing p. 90.
Thomas Bodkin, "A Rediscovered Picture by
 Nicolas Poussin," *The Burlington Magazine,*
 June 1939, pp. 254-259.
Painting and Sculpture, The Hermitage State
 Museum, Leningrad, 1939, pl. 15.
*Catalogue of the ... Barber Institute of Fine
 Arts, University of Birmingham,* Cambridge,
 1952, p. 82.
Fred Stephen Licht, *Die Entwicklung der Land-
 schaft in den Werken von Nicolas Poussin,*
 Basel, 1954, p. 110 (note 1).
Hermitage Catalogue, 1958, I, no. 1189, p. 326
 and fig. 254.
Sterling, 1958, p. 33, fig. 15.
Michel Alpatov, "Poussin peintre d'histoire,"
 *Actes du colloque international Nicolas
 Poussin,* Paris, 1960, I, p. 192.
André Chastel, *Nicolas Poussin,* Paris, 1960,
 I, pp. 192, 219, figs. 169, 171.

Nicolas Poussin

In the background at the right lies the slain Argantes. The gleaming white horse, which intently observes the action, sets off the dominant figure of Erminia and counterbalances the dark horse on the left.

Painted about 1631, *Tancred and Erminia* is an outstanding example of the influence of Titian on Poussin during his early career. The warm harmonies of the golds and browns, the transparent shadows, and the highlights on the armor show a love of color and sensuous handling of paint which Poussin derived from the Venetian master.

Poussin frequently painted second versions of his subjects. Thus a few years after the Hermitage painting, he returned to the theme of Tancred and Erminia in a work now in the Barber Institute of Fine Arts, University of Birmingham (fig. 9). This picture, with its larger figures, tighter and more linear handling, and more complex composition, is closer to the heroic style of his mature works. The pictorial sensitivity and emotional tenderness found in the Hermitage painting are characteristic of only a brief period in Poussin's career; later these qualities were supplanted by the intellectual and formal rigor of his *maniera magnifica*.

D.L.

René Jullian, "Poussin et le Caravagisme," *Actes du colloque international Nicolas Poussin,* Paris, 1960, I, p. 230.

Denis Mahon, "Poussin's Early Development: An Alternative Hypothesis," *The Burlington Magazine,* July 1960, p. 299.

Anthony Blunt, "Poussin Studies XI: Some Addenda to the Poussin Number," *The Burlington Magazine,* September 1960, p. 400.

Descargues, 1961, p. 160.

Denis Mahon, "Poussiniana. Afterthoughts Arising from the Exhibition," *Gazette des Beaux-Arts,* July 1962, pp. 28-30.

Prokofiev, 1962, no. 19.

A. S. Glikman, *Nicolas Poussin,* Leningrad and Moscow, 1964, pp. 43, 44.

Walter Friedländer, *Nicolas Poussin. A New Approach,* New York, 1965, p. 51.

Levinson-Lessing, 1965, no. 54.

Kermit S. Champa, "Paris: From Russia with Love," *Arts Magazine,* September-October 1965, pp. 53, 55.

P. M. Grand, "The Russian Delegation to Paris," *Art News,* October 1965, p. 59.

Alexander Watt, "From Russia with Love for Art," *Studio International,* November 1965, p. 205.

Anthony Blunt, *The Paintings of Nicolas Poussin. A Critical Catalogue,* London, 1966, p. 142, no. 206.

Anthony Blunt, *Nicolas Poussin,* New York, 1967, p. 148, pl. 70.

Kurt Badt, *Die Kunst des Nicolas Poussin,* Cologne, 1969, pp. 32, 520-522, pl. 99.

Kuznetsov, 1972, no. 71, 72.

Novoselskaya, 1972, no. 19.

Jacques Thuillier, *L'Opera completa di Poussin,* Milan, 1974, no. 68.

Exhibitions:

Chefs-d'oeuvre de l'art français, Palais National des Arts, Paris, 1937, no. 112.

French Art, XVth to Early XXth Centuries, Hermitage, Leningrad, 1955.

French Art XIIth to XXth Centuries, Hermitage, Leningrad, 1956.

Exposition Nicolas Poussin, Louvre, Paris, 1960, no. 42.

Chefs-d'oeuvre de la peinture française dans les musées de l'Ermitage et de Moscou, Bordeaux, 1965, no. 11.

fig. 9. Poussin, *Tancred and Erminia,* late 1630's, Barber Institute of Fine Arts, University of Birmingham, England.

Detail of No. 7

Louis Le Nain

French: Laon 1593 (?) — Paris 1648

8. A Visit to Grandmother 1640's
Oil on canvas, 23 x 28¾ in. (58.3 x 72.9 cm.)

Louis Le Nain was the second of three brothers who were all painters. The oldest was Antoine (b. 1588?) and the youngest Mathieu (b. 1607). Living near the Flemish border, they probably studied for a time with an unidentified painter familiar with the works of Caravaggio. About 1630 they moved to Paris, where they continued to work together until the deaths of Antoine and Louis in 1648. Although the Le Nain brothers produced some religious works and portraits, their finest pictures were genre scenes depicting groups of peasants in compositions which are only incidentally narrative. Genre painting was not highly regarded in the France of Louis XIII and Cardinal Richelieu; nevertheless the Le Nains gained recognition and were admitted to the Academy when it was founded early in 1648. In the nineteenth century their paintings were admired by Courbet and Manet who, as a young artist, copied the Le Nains in the Louvre. Picasso also had the highest regard for the Le Nains whose works exerted a considerable influence on him during his Blue and Rose periods (*cf. Les Saltimbanques,* 1905, National Gallery, Washington).

The three brothers shared a house and workshop in Paris and are believed to have collaborated on their paintings. As the works are signed with the family name and only dated during a short period in the 1640's, scholars have had great difficulty distinguishing their individual artistic identities. Only Mathieu's independent works after 1648 are clearly recognizable.

Louis Le Nain seems, however, to have been the most talented of the brothers. It is possible that he made a trip to Rome, where the popular Dutch artist, Pieter van Laer, known as Bamboccio, may have influenced his choice of rustic subjects and use of a limited range of colors. Unlike Bamboccio and most other seventeenth century painters of low life, Le Nain did not sentimentalize his figures. They appear instead as sad, immobile beings bathed in a cool light that lends them a timeless air of quiet mystery and nobility.

In the so-called *Visit to Grandmother* there is a notable lack of any definable subject. Each figure is psychologically isolated and not one glance meets another. The characters seem to be chosen at random from the Le Nain repertoire and are set vertically in a frieze-like pattern leaving the upper third of the picture strangely empty. The old woman in profile occurs in three other paintings by Le Nain, *The Family of the Milkmaid* (Hermitage), *A Peasant Family* (Louvre, Paris) and *Grandmother's Room* (Musée des Beaux-Arts, Lille). The young woman with a baby and the flute player are also found in other Le Nain works. *A Visit to Grandmother* has a greater richness than most of the paintings attributed to Louis Le Nain. It is particularly notable for the complexity of the interior, the subtlety of the light, and the introduction of large areas of red into his normally subdued palette.

C.L.

Provenance:
Pierre Crozat, Paris, by 1755
Catherine II, 1772 for
The Hermitage

References:
Catalogue des tableaux du cabinet de M. Crozat, Baron de Thiers, Paris, 1755, p. 54.
Jules Champfleury, *Catalogue des tableaux des Le Nain, qui ont passé dans les ventes publiques de l'année 1755 à 1853,* Brussels, 1861, p. 2.
Waagen, 1864, p. 303, no. 1494.
L. Clément de Ris, "Le Musée de l'Ermitage à Saint-Pétersbourg," *Gazette des Beaux-Arts,* March 1880, pp. 267, 268.
Somof, 1903, p. 66, no. 1494, and p. 67.
Antony Valabregue, *Les Frères Le Nain,* Paris, 1904, p. 171.
Sir Robert Witt, *Illustrated Catalogue of Pictures by The Brothers Le Nain,* London, 1910, pp. 12, 13, 34.
Benois, 1911, pp. 145, 146.
Serge Ernst, "Les Oeuvres des frères Le Nain en Russie," *Gazette des Beaux-Arts,* May 1926, pp. 303-305.
Réau, 1929, no. 195, p. 40.
Paul Fierens, *Les Le Nain,* Paris, 1933, no. 25, p. 61, and pl. XXXIX.
M. Lazarev, *Les Frères Le Nain,* Moscow, 1936, pp. 41-48, pl. 20.
Georges Isarlo, "Les Trois Le Nain et leur suite," *La Renaissance,* Paris, March 1938, pp. 5, 42, no. 75.
Hermitage Catalogue, 1958, I, no. 1172, p. 301, and fig. 225, p. 302.
Sterling, 1958, p. 18, no. 6 and pp. 22-23.
Descargues, 1961, pp. 154, 155.
Prokofiev, 1962, no. 12.
J. Thuillier, "Documents pour servir à l'étude des frères Le Nain," *Bulletin de la Société de l'Histoire de l'Art Français,* 1963, p. 187, note 1.
Levinson-Lessing, 1965, no. 52
Margret Stuffmann, "Les Tableaux de la collection de Pierre Crozat," *Gazette des Beaux-Arts,* July-September 1968, p. 110, no. 436.
Kuznetsov, 1967, no. 26.
Kuznetsov, 1972, no. 57.
M. S. Kagan, *The Brothers Le Nain: Antoine, Louis, Mathieu,* Moscow, 1972, pp. 11-13.

Exhibitions:
Le Nain, Petit Palais, Paris, 1934, no. 18.
French Art, XVth to Early XXth Centuries, Hermitage, Leningrad, 1955.
French Art, XIIth to XXth Centuries, Hermitage, Leningrad, 1956.
Chefs-d'oeuvre de la peinture française dans les musées de l'Ermitage et de Moscou, Bordeaux, 1965, no. 5.

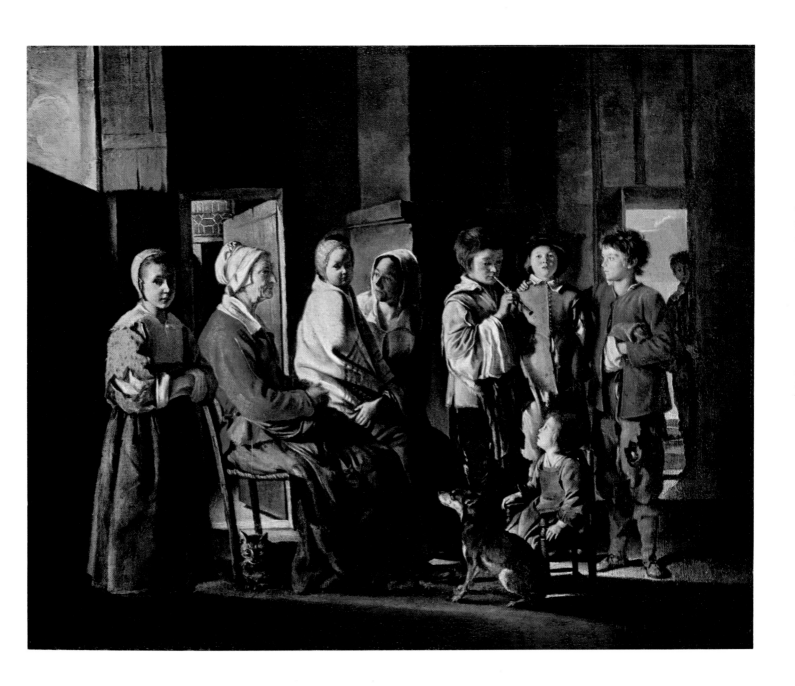

Claude Gellée called Claude Lorrain

French: Chamagne 1600 — Rome 1682

9. Landscape with the Rest on the Flight into Egypt 1661
Oil on canvas, 44½ x 61⅝ in. (113 x 156.5 cm.)
Signed and dated lower right below the Virgin:
CLAUDIO.IVF.ROM[AE] 1661

Born in Lorraine, Claude travelled to Rome about 1613 and studied there with the landscape painter Agostino Tassi. In 1625 he returned to Nancy, the capital of Lorraine, but by 1627 he was back in Rome where he remained until his death. About 1634, in order to guard against forgeries of his already popular works, Claude began his *Liber Veritatis,* a record book (now in the British Museum) containing drawings after his paintings.

Claude created a highly personal type of "ideal" landscape evoking an idyllic and nostalgic view of the past, unlike the more austere and heroic works of his close friend, Poussin. Claude's ability to animate a landscape with light and atmosphere was without precedent and his style had a lasting influence on later landscape painters of all schools.

The *Landscape with the Rest on the Flight into Egypt* (*Liber Veritatis,* No. 154) is one of four landscapes with religious subjects (all in the Hermitage) painted over a period of several years for an Antwerp collector. It was once believed that this group represented the four times of day, and that this particular painting depicted noon. Röthlisberger (1961), however, found no justification for this identification, observing that the light in the paintings does not correspond to the four times of day and that Claude, in any case, is not known ever to have painted such a cycle. According to Röthlisberger, they were conceived as pairs which are contrasted in composition but related in subject. The pendant to the *Landscape with the Rest on the Flight into Egypt* is the *Landscape with Tobias and the Angel.*

This painting captures a mood of pastoral tranquillity, as the Holy Family pauses on their hasty journey to Egypt to escape the massacre of the innocents ordered by King Herod (Matthew 2:13-16). The setting is a rich green countryside in which sheep and goats graze and men go about their daily occupations ignorant of the significance of the travellers and unaware of the miraculous presence of their guardian angel. The ruined temple is intended to suggest the triumph of Christianity over the pagan world. The Holy Family and angel dominate the composition despite their small scale. Claude accomplishes this through the use of the vivid blue of the Virgin's dress and the white of the angel's wings and robe. This creates a subtle contrast with the landscape which is enveloped in the cool light and limpid atmosphere of the Roman *campagna*. Here, as in most of his paintings, Claude did not attempt to represent any specific place but rather to create a vision of a past time when there was perfect harmony between man and nature.

Three preparatory drawings (Boymans-Van Beuningen Museum, Rotterdam; British Museum; and Albertina, Vienna) are known for this landscape scene.

D.L.

Provenance:
Commissioned by Henri van Halmale (d. 1676), Antwerp
Counts and princesses of Hesse-Cassel, Cassel (18th century).
Empress Josephine, Malmaison, 1806.
The Hermitage, 1815.

References:
Liber Veritatis or a Collection of Prints after the Original Designs of Claude Le Lorrain . . . , London, 1777, II, p. 6, no. 154.
Charles Blanc, *Histoire des Peintres de toutes les écoles. Ecole Française,* Paris, 1862, I, p. 14.
Waagen, 1864, p. 294, no. 1429.
L. Dussieux, *Les Artistes Français à l'Etranger,* Paris and Lyon, 1876, p. 579.
L. Clément de Ris, "Musée impérial de l'Ermitage à Saint-Pétersbourg," *Gazette des Beaux-Arts,* March 1880, p. 264.
Mme. Mark Pattison, *Claude Lorrain. Sa Vie et ses oeuvres,* Paris, 1884, p. 245, no. 1429.
Owen J. Dullea, *Claude Gellée Le Lorrain,* New York, 1887, pp. 132, 115, no. 154.
Somof, 1903, p. 37, no. 1429.
Masters in Art. A Series of Illustrated Monographs. Claude Lorrain, Boston, September 1905, p. 376, pl. VIII.
Edward Dillon, *Claude,* London, 1905, pp. 173-4.
Wrangell, 1909, p. 211.
Louis Réau, "La Galerie de Tableaux de l'Ermitage et la collection Semenov," *Gazette des Beaux-Arts,* November 1912, p. 395.
Walter Friedländer, *Claude Lorrain,* Berlin, 1921, pp. 90-96.
Weiner, 1923, pp. 282, 321.
Réau, 1929, p. 42.
Pierre Courthion. *Claude Gellée dit Le Lorrain,* Paris, 1932, pls. LVIII, LIX, and p. 186.
George Mihan, "Masterpieces Collected for the Hermitage by Catherine II and her Successors," *Apollo,* April 1944, p. 91.
Hermitage Catalogue, 1958, I, p. 305, no. 1235.
Sterling, 1958, pp. 29-30.
Descargues, 1961, p. 56.
Marcel Röthlisberger, *Claude Lorrain. The Paintings,* New Haven, 1961, I, pp. 361-5; II, fig. 258.
Levinson-Lessing, 1965, no. 61.
Marcel Röthlisberger, *Claude Lorrain. The Drawings. Catalog,* Berkeley and Los Angeles, 1968, p. 319, nos. 853-7.
Kuznetsov, 1972, no. 60.
Novoselskaya, 1972, p. 20.

François Boucher

French: Paris 1703 — Paris 1770

10. Landscape Near Beauvais *ca.* 1742
Oil on canvas, 18⅝ x 22⅞ in. (47.3 x 58 cm.)

Boucher received his initial training from his father, an embroidery designer. Around 1720 he entered the studio of François Le Moyne and, shortly afterwards, that of the engraver Jean-François Cars for whom he executed illustrations and decorative designs for books. In his early years he also made more than one hundred etchings after drawings by Watteau for Jean de Jullienne, a passionate collector of Watteau's work. In 1727, four years after winning the *Prix de Rome* at the Academy, Boucher went to Rome, where he remained until his return to Paris in 1731.

The turning point in Boucher's career came in 1734, when he was made a member of the Academy and was also asked to make designs for the royal tapestry workshop at Beauvais directed by Jean-Baptiste Oudry. He quickly became one of the most popular artists in Paris, producing innumerable works for the court, nobility, and wealthy bourgeoisie. Despite the many demands on his time, Boucher was an excellent teacher and his studio attracted many young artists including Fragonard. His brilliant career culminated in 1765 with his appointment as *premier peintre du roi* and Director of the Academy.

Boucher's interest in landscape painting dates from the early 1730's. While traveling through the countryside on his many trips to the tapestry workshop of Beauvais, he made drawings of interesting sites and buildings which he then utilized in the landscapes painted in his Paris studio. Boucher's landscape style was not based solely on accurate observation. He was also influenced by the landscapes of such seventeenth century Dutch painters as Abraham Bloemaert. Breaking with the tradition of the classical French landscape perfected by Poussin and Claude with its carefully ordered structure and restrained mood, Boucher's landscapes are arranged in a seemingly haphazard manner and show buildings in a picturesque state of dilapidation. Nature—especially the blue-green trees and creeping vines— is so lush that it seems about to consume everything made by man.

The *Landscape Near Beauvais* is typical of Boucher's work of the early 1740's. Though probably inspired by an actual site, the landscape has been transformed to accord with his personal vision of nature. Despite its artifice, there are passages that are completely convincing in their observation and reveal the artist's superb draughtsmanship and handling of paint. Like Guardi, he developed a repertoire of motifs, which he could readily manipulate. The *Landscape Near Beauvais* reveals that Boucher is one of the great landscape painters of the eighteenth century.

There are two drawings (Rijksmuseum, Amsterdam and Alte Pinakothek, Munich) by Boucher, which include the distinctive round building with the steep pointed roof. The *Landscape Near Beauvais* was engraved in 1744 by Jacques-Philippe Le Bas.

D.L.

Provenance:
Lenoir Collection, Paris (mid-eighteenth century)
E. P. and M. S. Olive, St. Petersburg (early twentieth century)
acquired by
The Hermitage, 1923,
passed to the
Pushkin Museum of Fine Arts, Moscow, 1925,
returned to
The Hermitage, 1930

References:
Paul Mantz, *François Boucher,* Paris, 1880, pl. facing p. 91; p. 92.
Louis Auvray, *Dictionnaire général des artistes de l'école française,* Paris, 1882, I, p. 129.
André Michel, *F. Boucher,* Paris, 1886, pp. 47, 54.
Edmond and Jules de Goncourt, *L'Art du dix-huitième siècle,* Paris, 1896, I, p. 304.
Pierre de Nolhac, *François Boucher,* Paris, 1907, p. 41.
Haldane Macfall, *Boucher: The Man, His Times, His Art and His Significance,* London, 1908, p. 39.
A. Troubnikov and Serge Ernst, "The Collection of E. P. and M. S. Olive," (in Russian), *Starye Gody,* April-June 1916, pl. facing p. 4; pp. 6-8.
Maurice Fenaille, *François Boucher,* Paris, 1925, p. 56.
Jeanne Duportal, *La Gravure de portraits et de paysages,* Paris and Brussels, 1926, no. 91, pl. LIV.
Serge Ernst, "L'Exposition de peinture française des XVIIe et XVIIIe siècles au musée de l'Ermitage à Petrograd (1922-1925)," *Gazette des Beaux-Arts,* March, 1928, p. 179.
Hermitage Catalogue, 1958, I, no. 5734, p. 261; fig. 181.
J. Q. van Regteren Altena, "Het Landschap bij Beauvais van François Boucher," *Bulletin van het Rijksmuseum,* 1959, no. 2, pp. 27-31.
Le Dessin français dans les collections hollandaises, Paris and Amsterdam, 1964, no. 82, pl. 66.
Levinson-Lessing, 1965, no. 72.
E. F. Kozhina, *Art in France in the 18th Century,* (in Russian), Leningrad, 1971, p. 46.

Exhibitions:
Possibly in the *Salon of 1742,* no. 19.
French Art, XVth to Early XXth Centuries, Hermitage, Leningrad, 1955.
French Art, XIIth to XXth Centuries, Hermitage, Leningrad, 1956.
François Boucher, Hermitage, Leningrad, 1970, no. 1.

Jean-Honoré Fragonard

French: Grasse 1732 — Paris 1806

11. The Stolen Kiss (Le Baiser à la dérobée) 1780's
Oil on canvas, 17¾ x 21½ in. (45.1 x 54.8 cm.)

Fragonard probably came to Paris in 1738. After a brief apprenticeship with Chardin, he entered the studio of Boucher about 1748, remaining there until 1752, when he won the *Prix de Rome.* For the next three years he attended the *Ecole Royale des Elèves Protégés,* which prepared young artists for their studies at the French Academy in Rome. From late 1756 until his return to Paris in the fall of 1761, Fragonard was in Italy, studying at the Academy and travelling with his friend and patron, the Abbé de Saint-Non.

In 1765 Fragonard submitted a painting as his *morceau d'agrément* to the Royal Academy in Paris, the initial step for admission into the Academy. He never, however, became an Academician but chose instead to work for wealthy patrons among the nobility and *haute bourgeoisie.* The popularity of Fragonard's works even upon the eve of the Revolution is indicated by the many engravings after them. During the Revolution, the support of his friend, the painter David, won him a position, which he held for six years, on the committee to form a national art museum. In his last years Fragonard seems to have painted little.

Fragonard worked in a variety of styles depending upon the subject and nature of his commission. His portraits, for example, are extremely free in execution with the paint applied in quick strokes and long flowing ribbons of color. Genre paintings such as the famous *Swing* (Wallace Collection, London) commissioned by the Baron de Saint-Julien or *Le Baiser à la dérobée* often reveal a more detailed and finished manner.

Because he could work simultaneously in different styles and rarely dated his paintings, the chronology of Fragonard's *oeuvre* is difficult to establish. *Le Baiser à la dérobée* would seem to date from the 1780's when Fragonard adopted the meticulous technique of such Dutch masters as Ter Borch and Metsu. It was engraved in 1788 by Regnault as a pendant to *Le Verrou* (Louvre, Paris, fig. 10), a painting by Fragonard which, though engraved in 1784, must be dated for stylistic reasons about 1775-80. It is unlikely that *Le Baiser à la dérobée* (fig. 12) and *Le Verrou* were actually painted as pendants. Aside from their disparity in size, the difference in technique and styles indicates that the former was executed several years later. There is furthermore no similarity between the couples who are represented, the décor of the rooms, or the emotional content of the two pictures. The overt passion which permeates *Le Verrou*—the forceful embrace of the man, the rumpled bed cover, and the overturned chair—is in complete contrast to the delicate and restrained mood of the Hermitage painting.

Much closer in spirit to *Le Baiser à la dérobée* is *Le Contrat* another Fragonard painting (now lost) which was engraved in 1792 (fig.13), also as a pendant to *Le Verrou.* Rosenberg and Compin (1974) observed that in the engraving of this lost picture there are on the rear wall two framed prints or drawings. One is of *Le Verrou,* the other of *L'Armoire,* an etching by

Provenance:
Stanislas Augustus Poniatowski, King of
   Poland (1732-1798)
Laziensky Palace, Warsaw, 1851
Acquired by Nicholas II in 1895 for
The Hermitage

References:
C. P. Landon, *Annales du Musée et de l'école
   moderne des Beaux-Arts. Salon de 1808,*
   Paris, 1808, I, p. 9.
Charles Blanc, *Histoire des Peintres de toutes
   les écoles. Ecole française,* Paris, 1862, II,
   p. 10 of the chapter entitled "Jean- Honoré
   Fragonard."
L. Dussieux, *Les Artistes Français à l'Etranger,*
   Paris and Lyon, 1876, p. 533.
Baron Roger Portalis, *Honoré Fragonard. Sa vie
   et son oeuvre,* Paris, 1889, I, p. 72; II, p. 271.
Virgile Josz, *Fragonard,* Paris, 1901, p. 119.
Ralph Nevill, "Jean-Honoré Fragonard, *"The
   Burlington Magazine,* December 1903, p. 290.
Somof, 1903, p. 36, no. 1845.
Edmond and Jules de Goncourt, *L'Art du
   dix-huitième siècle,* Paris, 1906, III,
   pp. 237, 285.
Pierre de Nolhoc, *J.-H. Fragonard. 1732-1806,*
   Paris, 1906, facing p. 124.
Armand Dayot, "Chardin and Fragonard," *L'Art
   et les artistes,* no. 27, 1907, p. 151.
L. de Fourcaud, "Honoré Fragonard," *La Revue
   de l'art,* April 1907, no. 121 between pp. 300-1.
Wrangell, 1909, p. 237.
Benois, 1911, p. 169.
Armand Dayot, *La Peinture Française au
   XVIIIe siècle,* Paris, 1911, pp. 216, 218.
Louis Réau, "La Galerie de Tableaux de
   l'Ermitage et la collection Semenov,"
   Gazette des Beaux-Arts, November, 1912,
   p. 396.
Georges Grappe, *H. Fragonard. Peintre de
   l'amour au XVIIIme siècle,* Paris, 1913, II,
   pp. 28, 56-7.
Louis Dimier, *Histoire de la peinture française
   au XIXe siècle. 1793-1903,* Paris, 1914, p. 32.
Weiner, 1923, p. 303.
Sir Martin Conway, *Art Treasures in Soviet
   Russia,* London, 1925, p. 169.
Louis Réau, *Histoire de la peinture française
   au XVIIIe siècle,* Paris and Brussels, 1926, II,
   pl. XII and p. 28.
Georges Grappe, *La Vie et l'Oeuvre de
   J.-H. Fragonard,* Paris, 1929, p. 217.
Réau, 1929, p. 28, no. 102.
R. H. Wilenski, *French Painting,* Boston, 1936,
   pl. 5 and pp. 155, 160.
Germain Bazin, "La Rétrospective d'Art
   Français," *L'Amour de l'Art,* May 1937,
   p. 22, fig. 43.
René Huyghe, *La Peinture française, XVIIIme et
   XIXme siècles,* Paris, 1937 (?), no. 18 and
   pl. XVIII.

Jean-Honoré Fragonard

Fragonard of 1778 (fig. 11) which shows a couple who have been discovered hiding in a large wardrobe. Fragonard's intention may have been to contrast in two pairs of works two different kinds of love and their consequences. Unrestrained passion *(Le Verrou)* results in discovery and humiliation *(L'Armoire),* whereas the control of desire *(Le Baiser à la dérobée)* leads to a stable relationship that is sealed by marriage *(Le Contrat).*

    Le Baiser à la dérobée effectively captures the tension felt by the young girl who desires to meet with her lover, yet is apprehensive about being discovered by the card-players in the adjoining room. Clandestine meetings of lovers were a popular subject in French eighteenth century art, but few artists could equal Fragonard in his ability to invest the familiar theme with such compositional inventiveness and psychological insight.

D.L.

fig. 10.

fig. 11.

fig. 12.

fig. 13.

fig. 10. Fragonard, *Le Verrou, ca.*1775-80, Musée du Louvre, Paris.
fig. 11. Fragonard, *L'Armoire,* etching, 1778.
fig. 12. Fragonard, *Le Baiser à la dérobée,* 1780's, Hermitage, Leningrad.
fig. 13. After Fragonard, *Le Contrat,* engraving, 1792.

Waldemar George, "La Femme, Mésure de l'Art français. La Peinture," *L'Art et les Artistes,* Paris, February, 1938, p. 160.
Painting and Sculpture, The Hermitage, Leningrad, 1939, no. 16.
George Mihan, "Masterpieces Collected for the Hermitage by Catherine II and Her Successors," *Apollo,* April 1944, p. 111.
Louis Guimbaud, *Fragonard,* Paris, 1947, p. 53.
Louis Réau, *Fragonard. Sa Vie et Son Oeuvre,* Brussels, 1956, pp. 52, 70, 108, 157, fig. 59;
Hermitage Catalogue, 1958, I, p. 346, no. 1300; p. 350, fig. 277.
Sterling, 1958, p. 53, pl. 45.
Georges Wildenstein, *The Paintings of Fragonard,* London, 1960, p. 320, no. 523 and pl. 124.
Descargues, 1961, pp. 176, 177.
René Huyghe, *L'Art et l'Homme,* Paris, 1961, III, p. 172, fig. 623.
Prokofiev, 1962, no. 74.
P. M. Grand, "The Russian Delegation to Paris," *Art News,* October, 1965, p. 60.
Levinson-Lessing, 1965, pp. 82, 83.
Alexander Watt, "From Russia with Love for Art," *Studio International,* November 1965, p. 205.
Jacques Thuillier, *Fragonard,* Geneva, 1967, pp. 12, 54, 72-74.
Louis Guimbaud, "Fragonard. Le Peintre des Graces," *Jardin des Arts,* February 1968, p. 81.
Raymond Charmet, *French Paintings in Russian Museums,* New York, 1970, p. 25.
Kuznetsov, 1972, no. 80.
Novoselskaya, 1972, pl. 37.
Daniel Wildenstein and Gabriele Mandel, *L'Opera completa di Fragonard,* Milan, 1972, p. 110, no 546; p. 111, fig. 546.
Pierre Rosenberg and Isabelle Compin, "Quatre Nouveaux Fragonard au Louvre, II" *Revue du Louvre et des Musées de France,* 1974, nos. 4-5, pp. 274-275.

Exhibitions:
Chefs-d'Oeuvre de l'Art Français, Palais National des Arts, Paris, 1937, no. 165.
French Art XVth to early XXth Centuries, The Hermitage, Leningrad, 1955, no. 60.
French Art XIIth to XXth Centuries, The Hermitage, Leningrad, 1956, no. 60.
Chefs-d'oeuvre de la Peinture française dans les Musées de l'Ermitage et de Moscou, Musée de Bordeaux, 1965, no. 21.
De David à Delacroix: La Peinture française de 1774 à 1830, Grand Palais, Paris, 1975, no. 60.

Detail of No. 11

Jean-Baptiste-Siméon Chardin

French: Paris 1699 — Paris 1779

12. The Attributes of the Arts 1766
Oil on canvas, 44¼ x 55⅝ in. (112.5 x 141.3 cm.)
Signed and dated lower left: *Chardin 1766*

The son of a Parisian cabinet-maker, Chardin received his artistic training from two history painters, Pierre-Jacques Cazes (1676-1754) and Nöel-Nicolas Coypel (1690-1734). In the studio of Coypel, Chardin was employed to add the still life details to the master's paintings. Influenced first by Flemish and then by Dutch examples, Chardin soon became a successful independent painter of still lifes, and in 1728 was admitted to the Royal Academy. In the early 1730's he began producing genre paintings which extol the virtues of bourgeois, domestic life. Throughout his career he exhibited at the Salon of the Academy, of which he was made treasurer in 1755. He was also entrusted with the delicate task of hanging the pictures for their exhibitions. Towards the end of his life, a shift in public taste caused Chardin's work to fall out of favor, and his death in 1779 attracted little attention.

The Attributes of the Arts was commissioned by the Empress Catherine II for the conference room of the Academy of Fine Arts in St. Petersburg, possibly to be used as an overdoor. Various objects symbolizing the arts of painting, sculpture, and architecture, as well as the rewards of the artist are displayed upon a cabinet. Painting is represented by a palette, brushes and paint-box at the left, and architecture by the plans, square, and case of drafting tools. In the center is a plaster cast of Jean-Baptiste Pigalle's statue of *Mercury* (1744), which stands for sculpture. Chardin, who owned a cast of this popular work, had depicted it earlier in *L'Etude du Dessin,* known from an engraving of 1757, where it serves as the model for a young artist.

In the Hermitage painting the artist's rewards are indicated by gold and silver medals and the Order of Saint-Michel on its distinctive black ribbon. The inclusion of the latter may refer to Pigalle, who, three years after this painting was completed, became the first French sculptor to receive this honor. In fact, the contemporary biographer, d'Argenville, relates that Pigalle was actually offered the Saint-Michel in 1765, but refused it on the grounds that there were other sculptors more deserving of the honor. If this story is true, it would suggest that Chardin's inclusion of the Cross and the *Mercury* in this painting of 1766 was intended to commemorate Pigalle's talent as well as his modesty.

Because *The Attributes of the Arts* was an official commission, of a decorative nature, the handling is somewhat tighter and the objects are rendered with more detail than is usual with Chardin. Their seemingly random distribution actually conceals a carefully organized structure. Chardin has placed the books, ruler, square, and paint-box at an angle that leads the eye into the picture and focuses our attention on Pigalle's *Mercury*.

In 1766 Chardin executed a replica (Minneapolis Institute of Art) of the Hermitage painting, which he exhibited in the Salon of 1769.

D.L.

Provenance:
Commissioned by Catherine II for the Academy of Fine Arts, St. Petersburg, 1766
Exhibited in the Hermitage
Auctioned at the order of Nicholas I, 1854
Greuch Collection, late 19th-early 20th centuries
H. van der Pale Collection, near Oranienbaum
The Hermitage, 1926

References:
Charles Blanc, *Histoire des peintres de toutes les écoles. Ecole française,* II, Paris, 1862, p. 16 of the chapter entitled "Chardin."
Charles Normand, *J.-B. Siméon Chardin,* Paris, 1901, p. 36, 37 and 105.
Réau, 1929, p. 20, no. 34.
Georges Wildenstein, *Chardin,* Paris, 1933, p. 242, no. 1131.
Sterling, 1958, p. 45 and p. 56, pl. 35.
Hermitage Catalogue, 1958, I, p. 355, no. 5627; p. 353, pl. 279.
Descargues, 1961, pp. 63, 172-173.
Prokofiev, 1962, no. 54.
Levinson-Lessing, 1965, no. 79.
I. Kuznetsov, *West European Still Life Painting* (in Russian), Leningrad, 1966, pl. 85 and p. 206, no. 85.
Kuznetsov, 1967, no. 76.
Georges Wildenstein, *Chardin,* Greenwich, 1969, pp. 219-220, no. 343, fig. 157.
Raymond Charmet, *French Paintings in Russian Museums,* New York, 1970, pp. 9 and 20.
Armand Dayot and Jean Guiffrey, *J.-B. Siméon Chardin,* Paris (L'Edition d'Art, H. Piazza and Co.,) n.d., second part, p. 77.

Exhibitions:
French Art XVth to early XXth Centuries, The Hermitage, Leningrad, 1955, no. 61.
French Art XIIth to XXth Centuries, The Hermitage, Leningrad, 1956, no. 61.

53

Diego de Silva y Velázquez

Spanish: Seville 1599 — Madrid 1660

13. The Repast (Breakfast) *ca.* 1618
Oil on canvas, 42½ x 40 in. (107.9 x 101.6 cm.)

Diego Velázquez, the greatest Spanish artist of the seventeenth century, was born at a time when Seville was a flourishing city, receiving and absorbing cultural stimuli from all parts of Europe. Although Francisco Herrera the Elder may have been his first teacher, Francisco Pacheco, to whom he was apprenticed from 1611 until 1617, was the most important influence on his early formation. Pacheco, later to become Velázquez' father-in-law, was a scholar-painter in the Renaissance tradition and founder of an informal academy which was a meeting place for the foremost intellectual and artistic figures of Seville.

In 1616 Velázquez became an independent artist, and in 1622 he made his first trip to Madrid where he was able to study works by masters of the Italian Renaissance in the royal collection. During his second trip to the capital in 1623 he was appointed *Pintor Real* (Painter to the King) to the young Philip IV, whereupon his importance and fame grew rapidly. He never returned to his native region of Andalusia but stayed at court, a loyal servant and friend to the royal family.

Velázquez gained further knowledge of older traditions and other styles of painting through contact with Rubens in 1628-29 and two trips to Italy in 1629-31 and 1649-51. However, despite his admiration for Michelangelo, Raphael, and Titian, and his familiarity with the theoretical writings of Dürer, Alberti, and Vignola, his distinctive, personal style remained basically unchanged. On returning to Spain in 1631, he participated in large-scale decorative projects for the royal residences in and around Madrid, and executed a series of masterly portraits of the royal family and members of the court, including the famous depictions of dwarfs and jesters.

His masterpiece *Las Meninas* (Prado, Madrid) was completed in 1656. In it the artist himself is seen in his role of painter to the royal family, wearing on his doublet the coveted Cross of the Order of Santiago which was awarded to him by the King in 1660 and posthumously added to the painting.

Velázquez, unlike most Spanish painters of the seventeenth century, produced relatively few religious works. In addition to his portraits, he painted classical myths, historical scenes, and genre subjects. *The Repast* is an example of a type of genre painting popular in Seville in the early seventeenth century, the *bodegón*. This word now means a still life, but then it designated a composition with figures as well as food. Like other examples of such scenes by Velázquez *(e.g. The Old Woman Frying Eggs,* National Gallery, Edinburgh, and *The Water Seller,* Apsley House, London), it reveals that he was strongly influenced by the naturalistic style of Caravaggio at the beginning of his career. Both Pantorba (1955) and Steinberg (1965) believe the Hermitage painting is the earliest surviving work by the artist.

Bright illumination from the upper right creates sharp highlights on the faces of the two youths. A smile crosses the face of the one at the right,

Provenance:
The Tauride Palace (?), St. Petersburg
The Hermitage, by 1774

References:
Paul Lacroix, "Musée du palais de l'Ermitage sous le règne de Catherine II," (reprint of 1774 Hermitage catalogue), *Revue Universelle des Arts,* April—September 1861, p. 249, no. 633.
Somof, 1899, p. 189, no. 1849.
G. C. Williamson, "The Hermitage Collection at St. Petersburg," *The Connoisseur,* December 1907, p. 217.
Albert F. Calvert and C. Gasquoine Hartley, *Velázquez,* London and New York, 1908, pl. 7, pp. 29, 30, 182.
Wrangell, 1909, p. 44.
Benois, 1911, p. 130.
Louis Réau "La Galerie de tableaux de l'Ermitage et la collection Semenov," *Gazette des Beaux-Arts,* November 1912, p. 392.
Walter Gensel, *Velázquez, des Meisters Gemälde (Klassiker der Kunst),* third edition, Stuttgart and Berlin, 1914, p. 4.
Weiner, 1923, p. 82.
August L. Mayer, *Diego Velázquez,* Berlin, 1924, pp. 53, 54, fig. 12.
Juan Allende-Salazar, *Velázquez, des Meisters Gemälde (Klassiker der Kunst),* fourth edition, Stuttgart, Berlin and Leipzig, 1925, p. 2 and p. 273, note 2.
August L. Mayer, "Das Original der 'Küchenmagd' von Velázquez," *Der Cicerone,* 1927, p. 563.
Carl Justi, *Diego Velázquez und sein Jahrhundert,* Zurich, 1933, pl. 1.
August L. Mayer, *Velázquez: A Catalogue Raisonné of the Pictures and Drawings,* London, 1936, p. 28, no. 121 and pl. 43.
August L. Mayer, *Velázquez,* Paris, 1940, pl. 10.
Enrique Lafuente, *Velázquez, Complete Edition,* London and New York, 1943, p. 17, no. I, pl. I.
Elizabeth du Gué Trapier, *Velázquez,* New York, 1948, p. 73-74 and fig. 48.
Juan Antonio Gaya Nuño, *Carl Justi; Velázquez y su siglo: Revisión y apéndice después de Justi,* Madrid, 1953, p. 866, no. 1, and fig. 22.
F. J. Sanchez Canton and José Ortega y Gasset, *Velázquez,* New York, 1953, pl. 2 and p. L, fig. 2.
Bernardino de Pantorba, *La Vida y la obra de Velázquez,* Madrid, 1955, p. 63, no. 1, pl. 1.
T. Kaptereva, *Velázquez and Spanish Portraiture of the 17th Century,* (in Russian), Moscow, 1956, pp. 41-42.
Kurt Gerstenberg, *Diego Velázquez,* Munich, 1957, pp. 26-27, fig. 20.
Juan Antonio Gaya Nuño, *La Pintura española fuera de España,* Madrid, 1958, p. 317, no. 2810, pl. 159.

as he playfully gestures at his younger companion in the center, who seems to be offering the viewer a drink of wine from his upraised carafe. The boys are observed by a bearded, older man, who holds a root in his right hand; on the wall behind hang his collar, hat, and sword. The presentation of these ordinary, unidealized types reflects the appeal that lower class life exerted on Spanish artists and writers in the late sixteenth and early seventeenth centuries.

The still life on the table is notable for its precise representation of such diverse items as the dish of mussels, glass of wine, ripe pomegranates, and crusty bread. With their emphatic shadows these carefully placed objects form a harmonious composition and evoke a feeling of space. The painting of the paring knife, projecting toward the spectator, is a *tour de force* of illusionism. The mood of the picture, the careful construction, and the interaction between the figures display the beginnings of the subtlety and understated expressiveness that were to become the distinctive features of Velázquez' art.

There is a version of the Hermitage painting in the Museum of Fine Arts, Budapest, in which the central figure has been transformed into a girl. Mayer (1936) lists six additional copies by followers of Velázquez.

E.S.

Hermitage Catalogue, 1958, I, p. 224, no. 389, fig. 134.

Enrique Lafuente Ferrari, *Velázquez,* Geneva, 1960, p. 34.

X. Malitskaya, "The History Paintings and the 'Bodegones' of Velázquez," (in Russian), *Trudy (Travaux du Musée Pouchkine),* Moscow, 1960, pp. 215-16.

Descargues, 1961, pp. 148-149.

Antonio Gaya Nuño, "Peinture picaresque," *L'Oeil,* December, 1961, p. 56.

Cesar Pemán, "Acerca de los llamados 'almuerzos' velázqueños," *Archivo Español de Arte,* October-December, 1961, pl. I, pp. 303-311.

José López-Rey, *Velázquez: A Catalogue Raisonné of his Oeuvre,* London, 1963, p .160, no. 113, pl. 6.

José Camón Aznar, *Velázquez,* Madrid, 1964, I, pp. 195-197.

Ursula Feist, "Die Gemälde des Velázquez in der Eremitage," *Anschauung und Deutung: Willy Kurth zum 80. Geburtstag,* Berlin, 1964, fig. 2, pp. 20-21.

Levinson-Lessing, 1965, pls. 36, 37, 38.

I. Kuznetsov, *West European Still-Life Painting,* Leningrad and Moscow, 1966 (?), pl. 64.

Kuznetsov, 1972, no. 35.

Marianne Haraszti-Takács, "Quelques Problèmes des 'bodegones' de Velázquez," *Bulletin du Musée Hongrois des Beaux-Arts,* 1973, p. 21, note 1; p. 22, fig. 17; p. 35, note 24; pp. 46, 48.

fig. 14. Murillo, *A Girl Selling Fruit, ca.* 1661, Pushkin Museum, Moscow.

Detail of No. 13

Bartolomé Esteban Murillo

Spanish: Seville 1617 — Seville 1682

14. Boy with a Dog *ca.* 1661
Oil on canvas, 29¼ x 23¾ in. (74.2 x 60.5 cm.)

Few painters have attained such heights of popularity and then fallen so totally out of favor as Murillo. From the time of his earliest known works in the mid-1640's until his death in 1682, he painted devotional and genre pictures in a highly sentimentalized manner that appealed to a popular audience in his own time, and to a more discerning public in eighteenth and nineteenth century England and France.

With the advent of Impressionism, however, and a general shift in taste away from religious subject matter, Murillo's art went out of fashion. It is only recently that his mastery of color and composition has led to a renewed appreciation of his *oeuvre*.

Murillo's earliest works show the influence of both Zurbarán and Alonso Cano. Subsequently, when he made his first and only trip to Madrid in 1658, the luminosity of works by Rubens and the Venetian masters which he saw in the royal collections made a lasting impression upon him. He spent the rest of his life in Seville. Murillo's most productive years were those of the 1660's. During this time he painted altarpieces for the Cathedral of Seville and a series of the *Acts of Mercy* for the chapel of the Brotherhood of Charity of which he had become a member in 1665. The paintings executed at the end of his life, with their airy *sfumato* and pastel colors, anticipate the rococo.

Most of Murillo's works are difficult to date, but *Boy With a Dog* can be assigned to the early 1660's, when the painter began to employ light colors in place of his darker ones of the 1640's and 50's. Both this and its companion picture *A Girl Selling Fruit,* (Pushkin Museum, Moscow) (fig. 14), are characteristic of Murillo's genre style. In these and five other similar scenes of urchins in the Alte Pinakothek, Munich, there is hardly any indication of a setting. The children, though ragged and poor, inhabit an idealized world from which all traces of the pain and misery of real life have been eliminated. This bitter-sweet quality greatly pleased the late seventeenth century public, all too familiar with plague, famine, and war. In the following century Murillo's sentimentality continued to exert a strong influence, notably on Gainsborough in his so-called "fancy pictures." In the nineteenth century Manet, a great admirer of Spanish art, painted his own version of this composition (Private coll., Paris).

There is a striking contrast between Murillo's use of loose, fluid brush work to indicate the clothing of the boy and the more precise delineation of the basket and jug. In his careful treatment of these objects Murillo reveals his connection to the long tradition of Spanish still life painting as practiced by such artists as Sánchez Cotán and Zurbarán.

E.S.

Provenance:
Duc de Choiseul, Paris,
    purchased at the auction of the Duc de
    Choiseul's collection by Count Galitzine for
Catherine II, 1772
The Hermitage

References:
*Catalogue des tableaux . . . de Monseigneur le
    Duc de Choiseul, . . . en son hôtel, rue de
    Richelieu,* Paris, April 6-10, 1772, p. 37,
    no. 118.
Waagen, 1864, p. 111, no. 377.
L. Clément de Ris, "Musée impérial de
    l'Ermitage à Saint-Pétersbourg," *Gazette des
    Beaux-Arts,* April 1879, p. 347.
Charles B. Curtis, *Velázquez and Murillo,
    A Descriptive and Historical Catalogue . . .*
    London and New York, 1883, pp. 276, 277,
    no. 413.
Luis Alfonso, *Murillo, el hombre, el artista,
    las obras,* Barcelona, 1886, p. 216, no. 376.
Somof, 1899, p. 168, no. 377.
Wrangell, 1909, p. 58.
Benois, 1911, p. 125.
Louis Réau, "La Galerie de tableaux de
    l'Ermitage et la collection Semenov,"
    Gazette des Beaux-Arts, November 1912,
    p. 393.
The Work of Murillo (Classics in Art),
    New York, 1913, p. 207.
August L. Mayer, *Geschichte der spanischen
    Malerei,* II, Leipzig, 1913, p. 101.
August L. Mayer, *Murillo, des Meisters
    Gemälde (Klassiker der Kunst),* Stuttgart and
    Berlin, 1913, p. 207.
Weiner, 1923, p. 96.
Paul Lafond, *Murillo,* Paris, 1930, p. 94.
Christian Zervos, "A Propos de Manet," *Cahiers
    d'Art,* Nos. 8-10, 1932, p. 317, (in reverse).
Painting and Sculpture, The Hermitage State
    Museum, Leningrad, 1939, no. 7.
Antonio Muñoz, *Murillo,* Rome, 1942, pl. 20.
George Mihan, "Masterpieces Collected for the
    Hermitage by Catherine II and her
    Successors," *Apollo,* April 1944, p. 89.
Emile Dacier, "La Curiosité au XVIIIe siècle:
    Choiseul collectionneur," *Gazette des Beaux-
    Arts,* July-September 1949, p. 68, fig. 16,
    p. 74, note 22.
Hermitage Catalogue, 1958, I, p. 236, no. 386,
    fig. 148.
Juan Antonio Gaya Nuño, *La pintura española
    fuera de España,* Madrid, 1958, p. 243,
    no. 1870.
Bazin, 1958, p. 98, and p. 102, fig. 73.
Descargues, 1961, pp. 150, 151.
Levinson-Lessing, 1965, pls. 45, 46.
Rafael Pérez Delgado, *Murillo,* Madrid, 1972,
    p. 179.
Kuznetsov, 1972, no. 37.

Francisco de Zurbarán

Spanish: Fuente de Cantos 1598 — Madrid 1664

15. The Young Virgin Praying *ca.* 1660
Oil on canvas, 29⅛ x 21⅛ in. (74 x 53.6 cm.)

Francisco de Zurburán was Spain's quintessential religious painter. In his many early commissions for religious orders in and around Seville he developed a realistic style imbued with a strong feeling of mysticism. From Velázquez he adopted his use of chiaroscuro. His figures were plain and unidealized, tranquil and spiritual, yet animated by inner energy. Zurbarán's most productive years were the late 1630's and 40's. In 1634 he painted his only large-scale secular works, two battle pictures and the series of the *Labors of Hercules,* for the newly built palace of the *Buen Retiro* in Madrid. His cycle of paintings of 1639 illustrating the history of the Jeronimite Order for their monastery at Guadalupe in western Spain is an impressive and iconographically sophisticated achievement.

From about 1645 onward, the Spanish public began to change its taste in art; Zurbarán's stern monastic manner fell out of favor, while the more gentle style of his younger contemporary, Murillo, came to the fore. Zurbarán attempted to adapt to this new fashion in his later less severe works, many of which were produced for patrons from the provincial centers of South America. *The Young Virgin Praying,* of about 1660, typifies Zurbarán's response to the sentimental manner of Murillo. Jonathan Brown (1973) has pointed out that representations of the young Virgin Mary, pausing to pray in the midst of her sewing, were derived from medieval legends which enjoyed a revival in the seventeenth century. Zurbarán convincingly captures here the innocent piety of a child. There is a notable lack of narrative detail, especially when compared with an earlier (*ca.* 1632-3) version of the same subject in the Metropolitan Museum of Art, New York, which shows the young Virgin seated between two curtains, surrounded by angels, and with flowers and other objects on the floor. The simplicity of the Hermitage painting, by contrast, reinforces its piety. However, this piety does not prevent the artist from indulging his fondness for the painting of drapery. The delicate embroidery on the collar and cuffs is sharply delineated as is the subtle pattern on the green sewing pillow. The deep red of the Virgin's garment complements her creamy pinkish-white skin. The intense light on the white cloth is reminiscent of earlier works by Zurbarán in which highlights and color contrasts are also strong.

A second version of *The Young Virgin Praying* (Gómez Moreno coll., Madrid) differs in some details from the Hermitage composition, but evokes the same spirit of gentle devotion.

E.S.

Provenance:
W. G. Coesvelt, Amsterdam, from whom it was acquired by
The Hermitage, in 1814

References:
Waagen, 1864, p. 105, no. 348.
L. Clément de Ris, "Musée impérial de l'Ermitage à Saint-Pétersbourg," *Gazette des Beaux-Arts,* April 1879, p. 347.
Somof, 1899, p. 191, no. 328 (incorrect, should be no. 348).
Benois, 1911, p. 130.
Hugo Kehrer, *Francisco de Zurbarán,* Munich, 1918, pl. 80, pp. 124, 125.
Sir Martin Conway, *Art Treasures in Soviet Russia,* London, 1925, p. 152.
Juan Antonio Gaya Nuño, *Zurbarán* Barcelona, 1948, p. 47, no. 235.
Martin Soria, *The Paintings of Zurbarán,* London, 1955, p. 185, no. 211, pl. 92.
T. Kaptereva, *Velázquez and Spanish Portraiture of the 17th Century,* (in Russian), Moscow, 1956, p. 37.
Hermitage Catalogue, 1958, I, p. 250, no. 306, fig. 170.
Bazin, 1958, pl. 66, p. 94.
Juan Antonio Gaya Nuño, *La pintura española fuera de España,* Madrid 1958, p. 345, no. 3130.
Paul Guinard, *Zurbarán et les peintres espagnols de la vie monastique,* Paris, 1960, p. 212, no. 28, pl. 86.
Descargues, 1961, pp. 146, 147.
Ramón Torres Martín, *Zurbarán: el pintor gotico del siglo XVII,* Seville, 1963, no. 39a (I).
X. Malitzkaya, "Zurbarán en los museos rusos," *Archivo Español de Arte,* April-September 1964, pl. II, pp. 109, 110.
Kuznetsov, 1972, no. 34.
Jonathan Brown, *Francisco de Zurbarán,* New York, 1973, p. 94.

Exhibitions:
One Hundred Masterpieces from U.S.S.R. Museums, Tokyo and Kyoto, 1971, no. 47.

Peter Paul Rubens

Flemish: Siegen 1577 — Antwerp 1640

16. Landscape with a Wagon (La Charrette Embourbée) *ca.* 1618
Oil on panel transferred to canvas, 34⅛ x 50 in. (86.6 x 127 cm.)

Rubens was one of the most outstanding men of the seventeenth century. He achieved renown not only as an artist, but also as a scholar, collector, and diplomat. His family came from Germany to Antwerp about 1588. There he studied with several minor painters and became a member of the Guild of St. Luke in 1598. In 1600 he journeyed to Italy where he remained for eight years working primarily for the Duke of Mantua, but also spending time in Rome and making a visit to Spain in 1603. He returned to Antwerp late in 1608 and soon established a large workshop, which during the next three decades, produced a prodigious number of works under his direction. These included portraits, church commissions, and designs for books and triumphal entries for his native city, as well as many large-scale projects for the royal courts of Spain, France, and England.

Rubens first displayed an interest in landscape subjects during his Italian period, but his earliest group of pure landscape paintings, including this notable example in the Hermitage, seem to date from the years 1617-20. Before this time landscapes had usually been presented as balanced compositions evoking a mood of serenity. Rubens, however, made landscape truly baroque, conceiving them as turbulent, exciting worlds filled with movement and struggle.

In the *Landscape With a Wagon,* as in other of Rubens' early landscapes, such as *The Watering Place* (National Gallery, London) and *Landscape with Farm Girls and Cattle* (Prince of Liechtenstein coll., Vaduz), the scene is divided by a towering central mass composed of rocks, trees, and roots. In a reversal of the usual perspectival arrangement with a gradual, unified recession into space, the effect created here is one of imbalance. The horizon line on the right of this landscape is higher than that on the left, so that the whole composition has a momentum toward the lower left. This momentum is further emphasized not only by the direction of the large tree at the right, but also by the angle of the wagon and the diagonal accent of the wagoner's red shirt. All this movement, as well as the eerie light of approaching night, that has brought the bats out of their daytime abodes, dramatizes the plight of the wagoners who are trying to right their tipping cart and reach shelter before nightfall overtakes them. The marvelous effects of reflected moonlit sky and the small figures gathered about the glowing fire were probably adopted from the night scenes of the German painter Adam Elsheimer, whose works Rubens had seen and admired in Italy.

The same wagon appears in two other paintings by Rubens, *The Prodigal Son* (Royal Museum, Antwerp) and *Winter* (Windsor Castle), and there is a chalk drawing for it in the collection of the Duke of Devonshire at Chatsworth.

As with many of Rubens' landscapes, this work was painted on a number of joined wooden panels. Although it has since been transferred to canvas, the seams of these joins are still visible.   E.Z.

Provenance:
Eberhard Jabach, Paris (?)
D. Potter sale, The Hague, May 19, 1723 (?)
William Cadogan, 1st Baron and Earl Cadogan
Sir Robert Walpole, Earl of Orford, Houghton Hall by 1743, by descent to his grandson
George Walpole, 3rd Earl of Orford, from whom it was acquired in 1779 by Catherine II
The Hermitage

References:
Horace Walpole, *Aedes Walpolianae: or, a Description of the Collection of Pictures at Houghton Hall . . . ,* 2nd Edition, London, 1752, p. 87.
John Smith, *A Catalogue Raisonné of the Works of the most eminent Dutch, Flemish, and French Painters . . . ,* London, 1830, II, p. 157, no. 547.
Waagen, 1864, p. 143, no. 594.
L. Clément de Ris, "Musée impérial de l'Ermitage à Saint-Pétersbourg," *Gazette des Beaux-Arts,* June 1879, p. 579.
Max Rooses, *L'Oeuvre de P. P. Rubens,* Antwerp, 1890, IV, p. 369, no. 1178; pl. 336 (in reverse).
Emile Michel, *Rubens . . . ,* London and New York, 1899, I, p. 281; II, pp. 242, 243, 314.
Somof, 1901, pp. 371, 372, no. 594.
Benois, 1911, p. 223.
Rudolf Oldenbourg, *P. P. Rubens, des Meisters Gemälde (Klassiker der Kunst),* 4th, newly revised edition, Stuttgart, Berlin and Leipzig, 1921, p. 185.
Weiner, 1923, p. 234.
Charles J. Sterling, "Les Paysages de Rubens . . . ," *Travaux des étudiants . . . ,* Paris, 1928, pp. 186, 187, 192, 195, 196.
Jacob Burckhardt, *Rubens,* Vienna, 1938, pl. 76.
Rubens, Paintings and Drawings, New York, 1939, pl. 76.
Hans Gerhard Evers, *Rubens und sein Werk,* Brussels, 1944, pp. 176, 350 note 2.
Gustav Glück, *Die Landschaften von Peter Paul Rubens,* Vienna, 1945, pl. 7; pp. 18, 56, no. 7.
Erik Larsen, *P. P. Rubens,* Antwerp, 1952, p. 201, and pl. 160.
Yvonne Thiery, *Le Paysage flamand au XVIIᵉ siècle,* Paris and Brussels, 1953, p. 92.
Bazin, 1958, pp. 149, 238 note 206.
Hermitage Catalogue, 1958, II, p. 82, no. 480; p. 92, fig. 83.
Levinson-Lessing, 1962, pl. 7.
Kuznetsov, 1967, no. 34.
Gregory Martin, *National Gallery Catalogues: The Flemish School,* London, 1970, pp. 208, 209.
Novoselskaya, 1972, pl. 16.

Anthony Van Dyck

Flemish: Antwerp 1599 — London 1641

17. A Family Group *ca.* 1620-21
Oil on canvas, 45 x 37⅛ in. (114.3 x 94.3 cm.)

Van Dyck was an artist of the utmost precocity. At the age of ten he became an apprentice to the painter Hendrick van Balen; at nineteen a member of the Antwerp Painters' Guild; and at twenty an associate of Rubens, who described him as his most talented assistant. In 1621 Van Dyck left Antwerp for a six-year sojourn in Italy where he worked primarily as a portraitist for the aristocratic families of Genoa; he also studied the art of the Italian Renaissance. He then returned to Antwerp, until invited to England in 1632. There he was knighted and made court painter to Charles I. Although he painted some religious and mythological subjects, Van Dyck is primarily famed for his elegant portraits of the English royal family and their court. These works established a standard of official portraiture for centuries to come.

Van Dyck's talent as a portraitist was already evident during his first Antwerp period. Around 1618-19 he adopted the type of intimate family portraiture that had been introduced by Cornelis de Vos, but he imbued it, as in this masterly *Family Group,* with his own distinctive qualities of vivacity and sensitivity. The faces of the adults intently regard the viewer, while the child, protectively sheltered by their hands, seems lost in reverie. The fluid style of painting is perfectly suited to the rendering of the rich clothes and setting favored by the Antwerp bourgeoisie.

The man in this *Family Group* was once thought to be the painter Frans Snyders, but comparison with Van Dyck's nearly contemporary portraits of Snyders and his wife (Frick Collection, New York) proves that this is not the case. The man does, however, bear a resemblance to another member of the Rubens' circle, the landscape painter Jan Wildens, who was portrayed several times by Van Dyck (Kunsthistorisches Museum, Vienna, and Staatliche Kunstammlungen, Kassel), and whose first child was born in August, 1620.

X-rays reveal that the man originally wore a mill-stone ruff similar to that of his wife. This was painted out, very possibly by Van Dyck himself, to conform to the taste for the flat lace collar which came into fashion about 1630.

E.Z.

Provenance:
M. La Live de Jully, Paris, 1764
Mme. Groenbloedt, Brussels, 1770
Catherine II, 1774
The Hermitage

References:
Catalogue historique du cabinet de peinture et sculpture française de M. de LaLive, Paris, 1764, pp. 114, 115.
J. H. Schnitzler, *Notice sur les principales tableaux de l'Ermitage,* 1828, p. 103.
John Smith, *Catalogue Raisonné . . .* London, III, 1831, p. 88, no. 300 and p. 300.
Charles Blanc. *Le Trésor de la curiosité,* Paris, 1857, p. 165.
Waagen, 1864, p. 149, no. 627.
J. Guiffrey, *Anthony Van Dyck,* London, 1896, p. 301, no. 847.
L. Cust, *Anthony Van Dyck,* London, 1900, pp. 18, 236, no. 56.
Somof, 1901, pp. 81, 82, no. 627.
Max Rooses, "Die flämische Meister in der Ermitage—Antoon Van Dyck," *Zeitschrift für bildende Kunst,* February 1904, p. 116.
H. Stokes, *Sir Anthony Van Dyck,* London, 1905, p. XLV.
Emil Schaeffer, *Van Dyck,* Stuttgart, 1909, no. 160, p. 501.
L. Dumont-Wilden, "Exposition de l'art belge," *Les Arts,* October 1910, pp. 15, 25.
L. Cust, *Anthony Van Dyck: A Further Study,* London, 1911, no. III.
Benois, 1911, p. 251.
Louis Réau, "La Galerie de tableaux de l'Ermitage et la collection Semenov," *Gazette des Beaux-Arts,* December 1912, p. 474.
Memorial de l'exposition d'art ancien à Bruxelles en 1910, Paris and Brussels, 1912, I, p. 148, pl. 57.
Wilhelm von Bode, *Die Meister der holländischen und vlämischen Malerschulen,* Leipzig, 1919, pp. 339, 350.
H. Fierens-Gavaert, *Van Dyck,* Paris, 1926 (?), p. 24, p. 29.
H. Rosenbaum, *Der junge Van Dyck,* Munich, 1928, p. 34.
Gustav Glück, *Van Dyck,* Stuttgart, 1931, no. 108.
A. Munoz, *Van Dyck,* Novara, 1943, pl. 13.
Bazin, 1958, pp. 152, 241, note 218.
Hermitage Catalogue, 1958, II, p. 52, no. 534.
Levinson-Lessing, 1962, no. 15.
M. Varshavskaya, *Van Dyck Paintings in the Hermitage,* (in Russian), Leningrad, 1963, pp. 100, 101, no. 5, pls. 10-15.
Kuznetsov, 1972, no. 41.

Exhibitions:
Trésors de l'art belge au XVIIe siècle, Nouveau Palais, Brussels, 1910, no. 66.
Terre des hommes, Expo 1967, Montreal, no. 65.

Rembrandt Harmensz. van Rijn

Dutch: Leiden 1606 — Amsterdam 1669

18. Saskia as Flora 1634
Oil on canvas, 49⅛ x 39½ in. (124.8 x 100.5 cm.)
Signed and dated lower left: *Rembrandt f. 1634*

Rembrandt van Rijn, who has rightly been called by Julius Held (1973) "the one great genius in a country teeming with men of talent" was the eighth of nine children born to a prosperous miller. He briefly attended the University of Leiden but soon left to study with the local painter Isaacsz. van Swanenburgh and then for six months with Pieter Lastman in Amsterdam, returning to Leiden as an independent master about 1625.

Rembrandt's works produced in Leiden reveal the seeds of his later development—an interest in Biblical subjects, self-portraits (of which he was to paint nearly a hundred), and the technique of etching. His earliest paintings show the influence of the forceful manner of Lastman and the dramatic color and light effects of the Utrecht Caravaggists. His later Leiden works, such as *Judas Returning the Thirty Pieces of Silver* of 1629 (Private coll., England), are more refined and intimate. This particular painting was praised by the contemporary connoisseur Constantin Huygens for its convincing expression of emotion, and such recognition led Rembrandt to make the decisive move to Amsterdam in 1631.

His first years there were marked by both artistic and personal success. He had the opportunity to study prints after the full-fledged baroque works of Rubens, and these enriched his art with a new grandeur. He began his career as a painter of individual and group portraits, including the remarkable *Anatomy Lesson of Dr. Tulp* (Mauritshuis, The Hague). The Prince of Orange commissioned a series of five Passion scenes, and in 1634 his marriage to Saskia van Uylenborch, the daughter of a wealthy burgomaster from Leeuwarden in Friesland, introduced Rembrandt to a new clientele of rich patrons and enabled him to begin his activities as a collector.

The decade of the 1640's was a transitional period for Rembrandt. His art began to reflect the classical influence of Italian masters such as Raphael and Titian. His rather dark manner of painting fell out of fashion and there was a consequent decrease in patronage. Nevertheless, Rembrandt continued to receive some major commissions—amongst which were a further group of works for the Prince of Orange and the so-called *Nightwatch* (Rijksmuseum, Amsterdam) painted in 1642, the same year as his wife's death.

During Rembrandt's last period, roughly 1648 to his death in 1669, his works became more personal in content and freer in style. He was influenced by the precepts of the Mennonite sect, and derived comfort and inspiration from his housekeeper-mistress Hendrickje Stoffels and the only surviving child of his marriage, his son Titus. After Rembrandt's increasing debts made it necessary for him to declare insolvency and liquidate his possessions in 1657-58, Hendrickje and Titus protected him by forming a partnership as art dealers with Rembrandt as their employee.

The deaths of Hendrickje in 1663 and Titus in 1668 were the final tragedies of Rembrandt's life. Yet despite these personal losses, his late works

Provenance:
Hermann Aarentz, Amsterdam, by 1770
Sale of the Aarentz collection de Winter and Yver, Amsterdam, April 11, 1770, no. 1 (bought in for 2,600 florins)
The Hermitage, 1775

References:
Catalogus van . . . Kabinet Schilderyen . . . door . . . Herman Aarentz, Amsterdam, April 11, 1770, no. 1.
Waagen, 1864, p. 181, no. 812.
C. Vosmaer, *Rembrandt, sa vie et ses oeuvres,* The Hague, 1877, pp. 504-5.
L. Clément de Ris, "Musée impérial de l'Ermitage à Saint-Pétersbourg," *Gazette des Beaux-Arts,* November 1879, p. 378.
Wilhelm Bode, *Studien zur Geschichte der holländischen Malerei,* Braunschweig, 1883, p. 424.
Emile Michel, *Rembrandt, sa vie, son oeuvre et son temps,* Paris, 1893, pp. 175, 179, 567.
Somof, 1901, no. 812, pp. 321-2.
Carl Neumann, *Rembrandt,* Berlin, 1902, p. 175, pl. 28.
Adolf Rosenberg, *Rembrandt,* Stuttgart, 1904, no. 85b.
Hermann Voss, "Rembrandt und Tizian," *Repertorium für Kunstwissenschaft,* 1905, p. 158.
Wilhelm R. Valentiner, *Rembrandt, des Meisters Gemälde (Klassiker der Kunst),* Stuttgart, 1908, p. 137.
Wrangell, 1909, p. 101.
C. Hofstede de Groot, *A Catalogue Raisonné of . . . Dutch Painters . . . ,* London, 1916, VI, no. 206, pp. 137-8.
Weiner, 1923, p. 125.
Carl Neumann, *Rembrandt,* Munich, 1924, I, p. 199 and fig. 40.
Sir Martin Conway, *Art Treasures in Soviet Russia,* London, 1925, p. 162.
Werner Weisbach, *Rembrandt,* Berlin, 1926, p. 235.
Otto Benesch, *Rembrandt, Werk und Forschung,* Vienna, 1935, p. 17.
M. V. Dobroklonski, *Rembrandt,* (in Russian), Leningrad, 1937, p. 9.
E. Kieser, "Uber Rembrandts Verhältnis zur Antike," *Zeitschrift für Kunstgeschichte,* 1941-2, p. 155.
Wolfgang Stechow, "Rembrandt and Titian," *The Art Quarterly,* Spring 1942, p. 145.
Richard Hamann, *Rembrandt,* Potsdam, 1948, pp. 215-6.
Jakob Rosenberg, *Rembrandt,* Cambridge, Mass., 1948, I, p. 43.
V. Levinson-Lessing, *Rembrandt Harmensz. van Rijn,* Leningrad, 1956, p. VIII, pl. 5.
Jakob Rosenberg, "The Rembrandt Exhibition in Amsterdam," *The Art Quarterly,* Winter 1956, p. 383.

in all fields display an unrivaled profundity of thought and expression. In self-portraiture there are such revealing examples as those at the Iveagh Bequest, London, and the National Gallery, Washington; in group portraits the *Syndics of the Cloth Drapers' Guild* (Rijksmuseum, Amsterdam); in historical painting the large *Oath of the Batavians* (National Museum, Stockholm), intended for the Amsterdam Town Hall but ultimately rejected; and in Biblical subjects such moving works as *Jacob Blessing the Sons of Joseph* (Staatliche Kunstsammlungen, Kassel) and the *Return of the Prodigal Son* (Hermitage).

Throughout his Amsterdam career Rembrandt was a teacher and made use of assistants. Among the many notable artists trained in his atelier were Gerard Dou, Carel Fabritius, Ferdinand Bol, and Aert de Gelder.

Saskia van Uylenborch, born on August 2, 1612, was probably introduced to Rembrandt by her cousin, Hendrik van Uylenborch, an Amsterdam art dealer. Saskia and Rembrandt were betrothed on June 5, 1633 and their marriage took place on June 22, 1634. Until her untimely death in 1642, Saskia served as Rembrandt's primary model for a variety of Biblical and mythological characters. From the first, however, she seems to have been associated in his mind with flowers and the regenerative power of nature, for in a drawing of her (Kupferstichkabinett, Berlin-Dahlem), inscribed by Rembrandt as having been made three days after their betrothal, Saskia already appears holding a flower and wearing a flower-encircled hat.

The Hermitage painting shows Saskia wearing embroidered and brocaded silk robes rendered in the highly finished manner typical of Rembrandt's work in the 1630's. She has flowers in her hair and carries a flower-entwined staff. A depiction of her in similar costume (National Gallery, London) was probably painted in the following year. Both paintings were once erroneously entitled *The Jewish Bride*. E. Michel (1893) was the first to suggest that they actually show Saskia in the guise of Flora, the Roman goddess of flowers and spring. Julius Held (1961) drew attention to the fact that in the best known classical account of Flora, Ovid's *Fasti,* she is described as "dressed in gowns of many colors" and that "when she shakes her hair, flowers fall from it."

Kenneth Clark (1939) proposed that, as there seems to be a cavern behind Saskia in this and the London painting, she may represent the mythological figure Persephone, the consort of Hades, who returned to the earth every spring and was often depicted strewing flowers. But there is no evidence that Rembrandt intended this cave or grotto to be the entrance to the underworld.

Neil Maclaren (1960) preferred to identify these works as Saskia dressed in the guise of an arcadian shepherdess. There was indeed, as Gudlaugsson (1958) and Louttit (1973) have shown, a seventeenth century pictorial tradition for the representation of real people in this type of costume inspired by popular pastoral plays such as P. Hooft's *Granide and Daphilo.* Rembrandt undoubtedly was familiar with examples of this tradition produced in Utrecht and may have adopted from them the Caravaggesque

Otto Benesch, *Rembrandt,* Geneva, 1957, p. 47, pl. p. 45.

Bazin, 1958, pp. 159, 244 (note 244), and fig. 147.

Hermitage Catalogue, 1958, II, p. 251, no. 732 and fig. 250.

N. Maclaren, *The Dutch School, National Gallery of London,* London, 1960, pp. 333-4.

C. Roger Marx, *Rembrandt,* New York, 1960, p. 158-60, no. 41 and pl. 41.

Napisala J. Michalkowa, *Rembrandt,* Warsaw, 1960, p. 82, pl. 55.

Descargues, 1961, pp. 130, 131.

Julius Held, "Flora, Goddess and Courtesan," *De artibus opuscula: Essays in Honor of Erwin Panofsky,* New York, 1961, pp. 207, 218.

Levinson-Lessing, 1962, no. 70-1.

E. Fechner, *Rembrandt, Paintings in Russian Museums* (in Russian), Leningrad, 1964, pp. 48-51, no. 6.

Jakob Rosenberg, *Rembrandt, Life and Work,* London, 1964, p. 72, pl. 61.

Pierre Descargues, *Rembrandt et Saskia à Amsterdam,* Paris, 1965, p. 96, pl. 97.

Seymour Slive, *Drawings of Rembrandt,* New York, 1965, II, no. 312.

Kurt Bauch, *Rembrandt Gemälde,* Berlin, 1966, no. 258.

Christopher White, *Rembrandt and His World,* New York, 1966, p. 32.

Kuznetsov, 1967, no. 56.

Horst Gerson, *Rembrandt Paintings,* Amsterdam, 1968, p. 246, fig. 92, and pl. 43.

Giovanni Arpino, *L'Opera pittorica completa di Rembrandt,* Milan, 1969, p. 103, no. 159.

Abraham Bredius, *Rembrandt, The Complete Edition of the Paintings,* revised by H. Gerson, London, 1969, p. 556, no. 102.

Bob Haak, *Rembrandt, His Life, His Work, His Time,* New York, 1969, p. 104, pl. 154.

Otto Benesch, "Caravaggism in the Drawings of Rembrandt," *Collected Writings,* I, London, 1970, p. 187.

V. Levinson-Lessing, K. Yegorova, I. Linnik and Y. Kuznetsov, *Rembrandt, Paintings from Soviet Museums,* Leningrad, 1971, p. 17, no. 7.

Kuznetsov, 1972, no. 54.

J. M. Nash, *The Age of Rembrandt and Vermeer,* New York, 1972, p. 36, pl. 54.

M. Louttit, "The Romantic Dress of Saskia van Uylenborch," *The Burlington Magazine,* May 1973, fig. 79, pp. 318, 322.

Exhibitions:

Rembrandt, Moscow and Leningrad, 1936, no. 5.

Rembrandt, Amsterdam and Rotterdam, 1956, no. 24.

Masterpieces of Rembrandt, Tokyo and Kyoto, 1968, no. 3.

Rembrandt, His Precursors and Followers, Hermitage, Leningrad, 1969, no. 6.

Detail of No. 18

device of a large, strongly lit three-quarter length figure set close to the viewer. But although they often have flowers in their hair, the shepherdesses in these earlier Dutch works have a vulgar, theatrical look. Rembrandt's Saskia, on the other hand, has the noble bearing of a goddess. Furthermore, the flower-entwined staff that she holds is, as Held has shown, a specific attribute of Flora. In this connection it is worth noting that when in 1636 Rembrandt's pupil Govert Flinck painted a pair of portraits depicting Rembrandt and Saskia as Granide and Daphilo (Rijksmuseum, Amsterdam and Herzog Anton Ulrich-Museum, Braunschweig), he copied the figure and pose of Saskia from Rembrandt's Hermitage painting, but substituted a plain staff, characteristic of arcadian shepherds, for the flowered one. That the subject of Flora was known to Rembrandt is proved by his notation on the back of a drawing of *Susanna and the Elders* (Kupferstichkabinett, Berlin-Dahlem) of *ca.* 1637, that he had sold two paintings of "Flora" by his students.

For all the nobility of Saskia's bearing, there is a voluptuous quality to her posture and gesture which accords with Flora's ambiguous role as a symbol of fertility and conception. Here she seems both to invite and fulfill erotic desires. The amplitude of her robes and her hand placed on her stomach, as well as the angle of the staff, indicate not only a fashion of dress but also symbolize the procreative urge. It may have been Rembrandt's way of invoking a fruitful future for himself and his young bride, although their first child was not born until December, 1635.

On the basis of the flowers that appear in Saskia's hair—ranunculus, anemones, frittilary, columbine, and tulip—the painting would seem to have been done in the spring, probably just before their marriage. Only rarely did Rembrandt pay such careful attention to a still life composed of elements taken from nature.

The London painting of *Saskia as Flora,* although presumably executed in 1635, shows a markedly older, fuller looking figure in a more frontal pose, leaning on a flowered staff and holding an assortment of flowers. A portrait of *Saskia Holding a Flower* (Gemäldegalerie, Dresden) dated 1641 has also sometimes been referred to as a *Flora*. Here too occurs the gesture of the hand on the breast, but the more open invitation of the offering of a single flower, probably derives from Titian's *Flora* (Uffizi, Florence), which in 1640 was in an Amsterdam collection.

About twenty years after painting the Hermitage *Saskia as Flora,* the artist paid homage to his second great love, Hendrickje Stoffels, by depicting her in the same role (Metropolitan Museum of Art, New York, fig. 15). Hendrickje too is turned to the left, has a large, and much more freely painted, arrangement of flowers on her head and wears a similar pearl drop earring. She seems to scatter flowers from the folds of her robe. The mood, however, has totally changed. No longer does Flora directly confront the viewer with an expectant and inviting gaze; instead she looks morosely to the side, as if caught in an almost painfully sad moment of introspection. For the aging Rembrandt both creation and life had taken on a somber aspect, far removed from the exuberant joy of his early married days. E.Z.

fig. 15. Rembrandt, *Hendrickje Stoffels as Flora, ca.* 1650, The Metropolitan Museum of Art, New York, Gift of Archer M. Huntington, 1926, in memory of his father, Collis P. Huntington.

Rembrandt Harmensz. van Rijn

19. The Condemnation of Haman (?) *ca.* 1665
Oil on canvas, 50 x 45¾ in. (127 x 116.1 cm.)
Signed lower right: *Rembrandt f.*

As Erwin Panofsky (1960) observed, the late Biblical works of Rembrandt contain "what may be called the eloquence of silence . . . all physical action is suppressed and only psychological situations remain." Rembrandt's process of condensation has made precise identification of some of these late works extremely difficult. Perhaps none has been more debated than this haunting work of about 1665 in the Hermitage. It depicts a large turbaned figure in the center foreground, who with a gesture of remorse seems to be taking leave of two other men placed behind a table. The one at the right wears a crown-topped turban and a golden chain and the other, at the left, is a sad old man. There is no visible communication between them; all three appear lost in private thoughts, shaken by some profound emotion.

A mezzotint by Richard Houston after the painting, published in 1772, bears the title *Haman's Condemnation.* This is a reference to an incident in the *Book of Esther.* Ahasuerus, King of Persia, had taken as his wife, Esther, a beautiful Jewess, who, on the advice of her cousin Mordecai, had not revealed her religion to the King. When the King's powerful courtier Haman, out of hatred for Mordecai, conceived a plot to have all the Jews of the kingdom put to death, Esther revealed her origins to the King and thus saved her people. At the end of the seventh chapter of the *Book of Esther,* the angry King orders that Haman be hung on the very gallows which the latter had prepared for Mordecai.

From the time of his early *Feast of Esther* (*ca.* 1625, North Carolina Museum of Art, Raleigh), the *Book of Esther* was a frequent source of inspiration to Rembrandt. The difficulty in identifying the subject of the Hermitage painting, however, is that not only is Esther, the heroine, absent, but the apparently reasonable identification of the three men as Haman in the center, the King at the right, and Mordecai at the left is contradicted by the fact that at no point in the Biblical text do all three characters meet. M. Kahr (1965) calling the work *The Downfall of Haman,* accordingly proposed that the figure at the left is not Mordecai but a servant and that the moment depicted is not the final condemnation of Haman but an earlier incident from chapter six of the *Book of Esther.* In this the King, after learning that Mordecai had once saved his life but had never been rewarded for his action, ordered Haman to go and honor him. Although the departure of Haman from the King at this moment is not described in the Bible, it does occur in Flavius Josephus' *Jewish Antiquities,* a book which was owned by Rembrandt. Josephus relates how Haman left the presence of the King "oppressed in spirit and stricken with helplessness."

Christien Tümpel (1967) also identified the scene as that from chapter six, but preferred the title *Haman Recognizes his Fate.* However, maintaining that the figure at the left is Mordecai, he attempted to demonstrate that Rembrandt had derived the composition and motifs such as the crowned

Provenance:
John Blackwood, London
Catherine II, 1769
The Hermitage

References:
Waagen, 1864, pp. 180, 181, no. 795.
W. Bode, *Studien zur Geschichte der holländischen Malerei,* Braunschweig, 1883, p. 479.
Emile Michel, *Rembrandt, His Life, His Work, His Time,* New York 1894, II, p. 245.
Somof, 1901, p. 309, no. 795.
C. Hofstede de Groot, *Beschreibendes Verzeichnis,* Paris, 1902, 7, no. 531.
Adolf Rosenberg, *Rembrandt,* Stuttgart, 1907, no. 247b.
G. C. Williamson, "The Hermitage Collection . . . ," *The Connoisseur,* December 1907, p. 210.
Wilhelm R. Valentiner, *Rembrandt, des Meisters Gemälde (Klassiker der Kunst),* Stuttgart, 1909, p. 469.
Wrangell, 1909, p. 117.
C. Hofstede de Groot, *Rembrandt Bibel,* Amsterdam, 1911, p. 102.
C. Hofstede de Groot, *Catalogue Raisonné of Dutch Painters . . . ,* London, 1916, VI, p. 49, no. 48.
W. Valentiner, *Rembrandt, Wiedergefundene Gemälde,* Stuttgart, 1921, p. 128.
F. Roh, *Holländische Malerei,* Jena, 1921, pp. 53-4, pl. 96.
J. Charrington, *A Catalogue of the Mezzotints after . . . Rembrandt,* Cambridge, 1923, p. 61, no. 81.
Weiner, 1923, p. 134.
Werner Weisbach, *Rembrandt,* Berlin, 1926, pp. 476, 594.
M. Eisler, *Der alte Rembrandt,* Vienna, 1927, p. 99.
M. V. Dobroklonski, *Rembrandt* (in Russian), Leningrad, 1937, p. 78.
Richard Hamann, *Rembrandt,* Potsdam, 1948, pp. 412-13.
G. Knuttel, *Rembrandt; De meester en zijn werk,* Amsterdam, 1956, p. 208.
V. Levinson-Lessing and I. Linnik, *Rembrandt van Rijn (Album),* Moscow, 1956, p. XIX.
I. Linnik, "On the Question of the Subject Matter of Rembrandt's Picture in the Hermitage," (in Russian), *Iskusstvo,* 1956, pp. 46-50.
A. B. de Vries, *Rembrandt,* Baarn, 1956, p. 68.
J. Bialostocki, "Ikonographische Forschungen zu Rembrandts Werk," *Münchner Jahrbuch der bildenden Kunst,* 1957, p. 210.
J. Bialostocki, "Recent Research: Russia II," *The Burlington Magazine,* December 1957, p. 422.
I. Linnik, "On the Subject of Rembrandt's Picture known as 'The Fall of Haman'", (in Russian), *Bulletin of the Hermitage,* 1957, pp. 8-11.

turban from engravings of the story of Esther by Galle after Heemskerck. But it should be noted that Rembrandt frequently made use of such crowned turbans to depict Biblical monarchs *(e.g., Belshazzar's Feast,* National Gallery, London; *David and Absalom,* Hermitage; and *Saul and David,* Mauritshuis, The Hague.)*

H. van de Wael (1969) presented the most convincing case to date for maintaining the old title of the painting, *Haman's Condemnation.* He identified the man at the left as Ahasuerus' chamberlain Harbonah, who in verse eight of chapter seven is the one who calls the King's attention to Haman's gallows and receives the instructions to "hang him thereon." He is thus logically the figure to be present at this moment of final condemnation, but as van de Wael demonstrated he is also a highly significant character, for according to Jewish traditions, which Rembrandt could well have known, Harbonah was actually supposed to have been the prophet Elijah in disguise, acting to protect God's chosen people, and as such his prominence in the picture seems justified, although his expression is hardly that of a victorious saviour.

The other identifications that have been made of this painting are all episodes from the life of King David, which also frequently served as a source of inspiration for Rembrandt. Valentiner (1921) and later Linnick (1956) and Bialostocki (1957) contended that it depicts the story of David and Uriah. As recounted in II Samuel 11-12, David fell in love with Bathsheba, the wife of the Hittite, Uriah, and sent the latter off to battle with instructions to his general that he be put in the front lines where he was quickly killed. For his callous action David was chastised by the Prophet Nathan. According to this interpretation the three men in the painting would be Uriah departing in the center, King David at the right, and the Prophet Nathan at the left. This reading of the painting seems unlikely, for in the Bible Nathan appears only after the death of Uriah. The alternative explanation that the figure at the left is the scribe of King David again does not accord with his obvious importance to the drama.

Valentiner (1957) proposed a new identification of the subject as *Jonathan Leaving the Banquet of King Saul* (I Samuel 20:24-34), but the central figure in the painting is certainly much too old to be Jonathan. A. Bader (1971) suggested another incident concerning Saul and David, *The Departure of David from Saul and Abner* (I Samuel 26:25), but in this instance there is no actual confrontation described in the Bible; their conversation occurs across a valley.

J. Nieuwstraten (1967) advanced the idea that the painting might be a fragment, but subsequent technical examination of the canvas, reported by Levinson-Lessing, Linnik, *et al.* (1971) revealed that it has not been cut at the sides.

While van de Wael's arguments for maintaining the title of the 1772 mezzotint, *Haman's Condemnation,* are the most convincing, any title must be left with a question mark, until a definitive identification of this subject can be made.

W. R. Valentiner, "Noch einmal 'Die Judenbraut'," *Festschrift Kurt Bauch,* Munich 1957, pp. 229-230.

Hermitage Catalogue, 1958, II, pp. 259, 264, no. 752; p. 262, fig. 259.

A. Tchlenov, "On the Subject of the Painting by Rembrandt, 'David and Uriah'", (in Russian), *Iskusstvo,* 1958, pp. 60-62.

Ludwig Goldscheider, *Rembrandt . . . ,* London, 1960, p. 185.

Descargues, 1961, p. 285.

Levinson-Lessing, 1962, pl. 84; (details) pls. 85-6.

E. Fechner, *Rembrandt, Paintings in Russian Museums,* (in Russian), Leningrad 1964, pp. 148-153.

Madlyn Kahr, "A Rembrandt Problem: Haman or Uriah?," *Journal of the Warburg and Courtauld Institutes,* 1965, pp. 258-273.

Kurt Bauch, *Rembrandt Gemälde,* Berlin, 1966, no. 39.

Kurt Bauch, "Ikonographischer Stil, zur Frage der Inhalte in Rembrandts Kunst," *Studien zur Kunstgeschichte,* Berlin, 1967, pp. 123 ff.

I. Nieuwstraten, "Haman, Rembrandt and Michelangelo," *Oud Holland,* 1967, pp. 61-3.

Madlyn Kahr, "Rembrandt's Meaning," *Oud Holland,* 1968, pp. 63-8.

Horst Gerson, *Rembrandt Paintings,* Amsterdam, 1968, p. 422, pl. 357.

Christien Tümpel, "Ikonographische Beiträge zu Rembrandt," *Jahrbuch der Hamburger Kunstsammlungen,* 1968, pp. 106-12.

Giovanni Arpino, *L'Opera pittorica completa di Rembrandt,* Milan, 1969, p. 123, no. 435.

Abraham Bredius, *Rembrandt, The Complete Edition of the Paintings,* revised by H. Gerson, London, 1969, p. 602, no. 531.

Julius Held, *Rembrandt's Aristotle and Other Rembrandt Studies,* Princeton, 1969, p. 30, pl. 36.

Erwin Panofsky, "Comments on Art and Reformation," in exhibition catalogue *Symbols in Transformation,* The Art Museum, Princeton University, 1969, p. 14.

H. van de Waal, "Rembrandt and the Feast of Purim," *Oud Holland,* 1969, pp. 199-223.

Alfred Bader, "A New Interpretation of Rembrandt's 'Disgrace of Haman'," *The Burlington Magazine,* August 1971, pp. 473-4.

V. Levinson-Lessing, K. Yegorova, I. Linnik, and Y. Kuznetsov, *Rembrandt, Paintings from Soviet Museums,* Leningrad, 1971, pp. 8, 27-28, 29, no. 29; pl. 29 (and three details).

J. Bialostocki, "Der Sünder als tragisher Held bei Rembrandt," in *Neue Beiträge zur Rembrandt-Forschung,* ed. by O. van Simson and J. Kelch, Berlin, 1973, pp. 138-40.

J. Bialostocki, "Rembrandt's Iconography," *Rembrandt After Three Hundred Years, A Symposium, October 22-24, 1969,* Art Institute of Chicago, 1973, p. 75.

Detail of No. 19

Rembrandt Harmensz.van Rijn

Rembrandt Harmensz.van Rijn

If the subject is problematic, there is no doubt about the power and effectiveness of Rembrandt's composition. His masterly rendering of both materials and emotions is nowhere more evident than in his painting of the central figure. He dominates the scene not only through his size, but because Rembrandt has intentionally made the spatial relationships between the figures equivocal. Furthermore the central figure calls attention to himself by his expressive *mea culpa* gesture, while the hands of the flanking figures are hidden from view. Also the guilty "Haman" has his eyes cast downward and his face nearly concealed by shadows, unlike the other two men who, although gazing abstractedly into space, are portrayed with open eyes and frank countenances. It is above all the expanse of "Haman's" sumptuous red robe and cape, contrasting so vividly with his anguished expression, that captures the viewer's eye. As Slive and Rosenberg (1972) have observed, color in Rembrandt's late works "becomes a living, moving substance which ebbs and flows through space . . . linking the subjects with their mysterious dark backgrounds and even with infinite space." Here indeed the red of the garments has a living quality and by overlapping the other figures manages to envelope them both physically and emotionally in the same truly mysterious and empty world, so that as Panofsky said, "the very difference between good and evil, triumph and defeat [is] submerged in a communion of muted sadness."

E.Z.

Julius Held and Donald Posner, *Seventeenth and Eighteenth Century Art,* New York, 1973, p. 266, pl. 276.

Exhibitions:
Rembrandt, Moscow and Leningrad, 1936, no. 27.
Rembrandt and His School, Moscow and Leningrad, 1956, no. 61.
Masterpieces of Rembrandt, Tokyo and Kyoto, 1968, no. 11.
Rembrandt, His Precursors and Followers, Hermitage, Leningrad, 1969, no. 23.

Detail of No. 19

Willem Claesz. Heda

Dutch: Haarlem (?) 1593/4 — Haarlem (?) 1680/2

20. Still Life with Crab 1648
Oil on canvas, 46 x 46 in. (117 x 117 cm.)
Signed and dated on the edge of the tablecloth: *Heda 1648*

Willem Claesz. Heda was, with his fellow Haarlem artist, Pieter Claesz., one of the most important representatives of the Dutch school of still life painters who specialized in what were known as *monochrome ontbijt* (monochrome breakfast-pieces). These typified a Dutch love for the display of beautiful, domestic objects and good food. Heda was enrolled as a member of the Haarlem Painters' Guild by 1631 and devoted his long career almost exclusively to the production of still lifes, employing repeatedly the same limited repertoire of familiar items. Since he frequently signed and dated his works, it is possible to observe a certain evolution in his style. His earliest dated paintings of the 1630's, such as a *Still Life with Nuts* (Louvre, Paris), are simple and rather severe in their grouping of objects. After 1640 Heda's work tends to become richer in content and more decorative. This tendency continues into the following decade, as his still lifes grow more lively and are painted somewhat more broadly. In the artist's last known works of the 1660's, the influence of the then popular Willem Kalf is evident in the use of richer colors and the introduction of new details such as Oriental rugs.

This work of 1648 contains many of Heda's usual still life elements, such as the ewer, the long-stemmed glass, and the filled *roemer* at the right. These and the other objects are all crowded close to the edge of the table and displayed against a bare wall. They are illuminated by a strong light which is reflected on the surfaces of the polished metal and glass. The most unusual item is the crab, which appears only rarely in Heda's breakfast pieces (*cf.* an example of 1634 in the Alte Pinakothek, Munich). It also figures, along with a composition similar in many respects to the Hermitage painting, in a *Still Life* (National Gallery, London), which is now attributed to the artist's son Gerrit.

Heda has here freed himself from the constraint of his first period. There is a definite sense of disorder in the rumpled tablecloth, fallen vessels, tipped plate of olives, and lemon skin curling off the edge of the table. As has often been observed, this still life has the appearance of a meal just begun and then abruptly abandoned. At the same time one feels it is a self-contained unit, complete and independent of any outside forces. Each object is animated by a life of its own, yet seems engaged in a frozen communion with its neighbors.

E.Z.

Provenance:
The Hermitage, 1920

References:
M. Shcherbacheva, *Still Life in Dutch Painting,* (in Russian), Leningrad, 1945, p. 20.
Hermitage Catalogue, 1958, II, p. 173, no. 5606.
Y. Kuznetsov, *West European Still-Life Painting,* Leningrad, 1966, pp. 177-8, no. 28.
Jakob Rosenberg, Seymour Slive and E. H. ter Kuile, *Dutch Art and Architecture: 1600-1800,* Baltimore, 1972, p. 337, pl. 266.
Kuznetsov, 1972, no. 51.

Additional Bibliography:
H. E. van Gelder, *W. C. Heda, A. van Beyeren, W. Kalf,* Amsterdam, 1941, pp. 9-20.
N. R. A. Vroom, *De Schilders van het Monochrome Banketje,* Amsterdam, 1945, pp. 55-87.
Ingvar Bergström, *Dutch Still Life Painting in the Seventeenth Century,* London, 1956, pp. 123-134.

Frans Hals

Dutch: Antwerp 1582 — Haarlem 1666

21. Portrait of a Man *ca.* 1651
Oil on canvas, 33¼ x 26⅝ in. (84.5 x 67 cm.)
Signed on the right with the monogram: *FH*

Frans Hals was the pre-eminent Dutch portrait painter of the seventeenth century. His family was established in Haarlem by 1591, and there he remained for the duration of his long career. He was a pupil of the artist-writer Karel van Mander, and in 1610 joined the Haarlem Guild of St. Luke as an independent master. His portraits, especially the large group studies, won him renown throughout Holland. Late in life, however, he apparently experienced some financial difficulties. His remarkable ability to capture directly on canvas the essence of his subjects' personalities with rapid brushwork of the utmost dash and virtuosity, often using a palette virtually limited to whites and blacks, made Hals a popular model for many nineteenth century painters, among them Courbet, Manet, and van Gogh.

This painting of an unknown man is a marvel of the artist's later period. Seymour Slive (1974) has called it "one of the finest of the great series of portraits Hals made in the early sixteen-fifties." In a pose characteristic of Hals' work at this time (*cf. The Portrait of a Man* in the Metropolitan Museum of Art, New York), the figure is turned slightly to the right and holds his right hand upon his hip as he haughtily regards the spectator. The large black bulk of his body and shirt is broken by the violent white strokes of the cuff. Hal's freedom of handling is nowhere better observed than in the summary rendering of the mustache and the treatment of the hair, which tumbles down in a torrent at the left and flies out at the right.

Most scholars now agree that the chalk drawing after this portrait in the British Museum (fig.16) is not by Hals but by an anonymous copyist. It reveals that the man originally wore a jaunty hat decorated with a pompom. In the Hermitage portrait this hat was painted out at a later date, but traces of it are still evident.

E.Z.

fig. 16.   Anonymous Copyist after Hal's *Portrait of a Man*, chalk drawing, British Museum, London.

Provenance:
Catherine II, acquired between 1763 and 1774
The Hermitage,

References:
Waagen, 1864, no. 772, p. 172.
Wilhelm von Bode, *Studien zur Geschichte der holländischen Malerei,* Braunschweig, 1883, p. 13.
Somof, 1901, no. 772, p. 140.
E. W. Moes, *Frans Hals, sa vie et son oeuvre,* Brussels, 1909, p. 108, no. 182.
Wrangell, 1909, p. 144.
C. Hofstede de Groot, *A Catalogue Raisonné of . . . Dutch Painters . . . ,* London, 1910, III, pp. 88-9, no. 309.
Wilhelm von Bode and M. J. Binder, *Frans Hals, sein Leben und seine Werke,* Berlin, 1914, II, no. 226, pl. 173b.
Wilhelm Reinhold Valentiner, *Frans Hals, (Klassiker der Kunst),* Stuttgart, 1921, p. 244.
Weiner, 1923, p. 116.
Max J. Friedländer, *Die niederländischen Maler der 17. Jahrhunderts,* Berlin, 1926, p. 166.
J. Q. van Regteren Altena, "Frans Hals Teekenaar," *Oud-Holland,* 1929, pp. 149-152.
Franz Dülberg, *Frans Hals. Ein Leben und ein Werk,* Stuttgart, 1930, p. 200, fig. 2.
N. S. Trivas, *The Painting of Frans Hals,* New York, 1941, no. 96, pl. 127.
J. Q. van Regteren Altena, *Dutch Master Drawings of the Seventeenth Century,* London, 1949, p. XXVII, no. 16.
Bazin, 1958, p. 243, note 237; fig. 139.
Hermitage Catalogue, 1958, II, p. 170, no. 816.
H. Fechner, " 'Portrait of a Man' by Frans Hals," *Bulletin of the Hermitage Museum* (in Russian), 1960, pp. 14-16.
Descargues, 1961, p. 282.
Levinson-Lessing, 1962, no. 28.
I. V. Linnik, *Frans Hals* (in Russian), 1967, no. 36.
Seymour Slive, *Frans Hals,* New York, 1970-4, I, pp. 191-3; II, pls. 299-300; III, pp. 100-101, no. 193.
C. Grimm, *Frans Hals,* Berlin, 1972, p. 111, no. 148, pls. 169, 171.
Kuznetsov, 1972, no. 47.
Novoselskaya, 1972, no. 23.
Jakob Rosenberg, Seymour Slive and E. H. ter Kuile, *Dutch Art and Architecture: 1600-1800,* Baltimore, 1972, p. 430.

Exhibitions:
Frans Hals, Frans Hals Museum, Haarlem, 1962, no. 79.

Gerard Ter Borch

Dutch: Zwolle 1617 — Deventer 1681

22. Portrait of a Woman (Catrina Leunink) *ca.* 1663
Oil on canvas, 31⅜ x 23¼ in. (79.6 x 59.1 cm.)

Ter Borch probably began to study art with his father, who was a painter until he accepted a post with the municipal treasury in 1621. In 1632 the young Ter Borch made his first visit to Amsterdam, and in 1634 he went to Haarlem, where he worked with the landscape painter Pieter de Molijn. On these trips he undoubtedly saw examples of early works by Hals and Rembrandt, but he himself at this time primarily painted scenes of military life, such as guardroom and tavern interiors. Ter Borch continued his travels: to England in 1635, and to Italy and possibly Spain in the 1640's. He was back at Amsterdam by 1645, but the following year visited Münster in Germany, where delegates were gathering for the Congress on the Peace of Europe. Here he remained for three years, receiving many commissions for his distinctive miniature-like portraits and ultimately painting his only known historical work, *The Peace of Münster* (National Gallery, London), which depicts the ceremony of ratifying the treaty which ended eighty years of war and granted independence to the United Provinces of the Netherlands. Among the participants present at this noteworthy event, Ter Borch included his own self-portrait. By 1650 Ter Borch was back in Holland, and from 1654 on was established at the small town of Deventer, where he remained a respected citizen until the time of his death. Aside from his portraits, of which about one hundred and seventy survive, he is best known as a genre painter of intimate scenes from daily Dutch life, in the manner of Metsu.

On the basis of a coat of arms on the back of this painting, Gudlaugsson (1959) identified the woman as Catrina Leunink, the wife of the Burgomaster of Deventer, Jan van Suchtelen. Also on the back of the painting is inscribed the date 1635. If this, as Gudlaugsson believed, is Catrina Leunink's birth date, her apparent age would seem to date the painting about 1662-3. Since Jan van Suchtelen received his first official position in 1663, it is very possible that he commissioned a pair of portraits from Ter Borch on this occasion. Such pairs of portraits, representing a husband and wife facing each other, were extremely popular in Holland during the seventeenth century. If there was a pendant, it is now lost.

In Gudlaugsson's opinion this painting may well be the first in which Ter Borch introduced what was to become his standard format for women's portraits: a small doll-like figure, isolated in the middle of the shadowed space of a bare room. From a triangular opening in her black over-dress gleams forth a brilliant under-dress of silk and gold brocade. This distracts the eye from her rather self-conscious gaze and slightly awkward pose. Through his use of color as well as his meticulous craftsmanship, Ter Borch managed to combine in his representations of such middle-class ladies both a mood of quiet reserve and a jewel-like delicacy.   E.Z.

Provenance:
Prince van Suchtelen (d. 1836), St. Petersburg
F. Kuchelev-Besborodko Collection,
  St. Petersburg, by 1886
Museum of the Academy of Fine Arts,
  Leningrad
The Hermitage, 1922

References:
Catalogue of the Kuchelev Gallery,
  St. Petersburg, 1886, no. 74.
C. Hofstede de Groot, *A Catalogue Raisonné of
  . . . Dutch Painters. . . ,* London, 1913, V,
  p. 124, no. 407.
A. Pappé, "Some Unpublished Dutch Pictures
  in the Hermitage," *The Burlington Magazine,*
  January 1925, p. 47, pl. p. 46 A.
Hermitage Catalogue, 1958, II, p. 279, no. 3783;
  fig. 275.
S. J. Gudlaugsson, *Gerard Ter Borch,* The
  Hague, 1959-60, I, p. 140, pl. p. 327; II, p. 182,
  no. 184.
Levinson-Lessing, 1962, no. 31.

Additional Bibliography:
E. W. Moes, "Gerard Ter Borch en zijne familie,"
  Oud Holland, IV, 1886, p. 148 ff.
Emile Michel, *Gerard Terburg et sa famille,*
  Paris, 1887.
Franz Hellens, *Gérard Terborch,* Brussels, 1911.
Frits Hannema, *Gerard Terborch,* Amsterdam,
  1943.
E. Plietzsch, *Gerard ter Borch,* Vienna, 1944.
Gerard Ter Borch (Exhibition Cat.), The Hague
  and Münster, 1974.

Exhibitions:
*One Hundred Masterpieces from U.S.S.R.
  Museums,* Tokyo and Kyoto, 1971, no. 46.

Jacob Van Ruisdael

Dutch: Haarlem 1628 — Haarlem 1682

23. A Forest Marsh *ca.* 1665
Oil on canvas, 28⅝ x 38¾ in. (72.8 x 98.5 cm.)
Signed lower right: *Jv. Ruisdael*

Jacob van Ruisdael was the most important member of a family of gifted artists. Indeed his father, Isaack Jacobsz., and his uncle, Salomon, both specialists in landscape painting, were probably his first teachers. He was later influenced by the waterfall and forest scenes of Vroom and Everdingen, but even in his earliest dated works of the 1640's, Ruisdael displayed a markedly individual spirit that is both poetic and serious. By 1648 he was a member of the Haarlem Painters' Guild and in 1657 he moved to Amsterdam. His interest in observing new landscapes took him on travels through Germany and Holland, sometimes in the company of another landscape painter Nicholaes Berchem. Late in life, after he had nearly abandoned painting, he returned to Haarlem. Of his many pupils the most important was Meindert Hobbema.

Jakob Rosenberg (1928) has written that, "Ruisdael was the only one of the Dutch landscape painters of the seventeenth century who had a fully developed feeling for the beauty and the unique qualities of the forest." This accolade applies unreservedly to the Hermitage's *Forest Marsh*. The still pond, covered with water lilies and encircled by huge oak trees, occurs in several of Ruisdael's other paintings of the mid-1660's (*cf.* examples in the National Gallery, London, and Staatliche Museen, Dahlem-Berlin). These were inspired by engravings of Egidius Sadeler after imaginary forest scenes by Roelant Savery, and possess the monumental grandeur typical of Ruisdael's finest works. But, unlike Savery's mannerist tangle of trunks and branches, his paintings suggest a real local. In the *Forest Marsh* there is a timeless calm and strength to the natural elements that dwarfs the figure of man and reveals him as an intruder in this still world. One readily senses here the artist's deeply felt response to the forces of nature, the processes of growth and decay and the interplay between earth, sky and water. The muted golden and russet hues further enhance the nobility of Ruisdael's conception.

E.Z.

Provenance:
Catherine II, acquired between 1763 and 1774
The Hermitage,

References:
Waagen, 1864, p. 387, no. 140.
Emile Michel, *Jacob van Ruysdael,* Paris, 1890, p. 60.
Frank Cundall, *The Landscape and Pastoral Painters of Holland: Ruisdael, Hobbema, Cuijp, Potter,* New York, 1891, p. 24.
Somof, 1901, no. 1136, p. 378.
Masters in Art. Ruisdael., Boston, 1907, pp. 79-80, pl. V.
Wrangell, 1909, p. 180.
Benois, 1911, p. 427.
Louis Réau, "La Galerie de tableaux de l'Ermitage et la collection Semenov," (deuxième article), *Gazette des Beaux-Arts,* December 1912, p. 483.
C. Hofstede de Groot, *A Catalogue Raisonné of Dutch Painters,* London, 1912, IV, pp. 159-160, no. 508.
Wilhelm von Bode, *Die Meister der holländischen und vlämischen Malerschulen,* Leipzig, 1919, p. 186.
Weiner, 1923, p. 171.
M. I. Shcherbacheva, "The New Installation of The Dutch Galleries at the Hermitage," (in Russian), *Sredi Kollekcionerov,* 1924, p. 21, no. 9-12.
Jakob Rosenberg, *Jacob van Ruisdael,* Berlin, 1928, pp. 48-49, 91, no. 313, pl. 103.
G. Riat, *Ruysdael,* Paris, 1928, pp. 103-107.
Karl Simon, *Jacob van Ruisdael,* Berlin, 1930, p. 46.
Horst Gerson, "The Development of Ruisdael," *The Burlington Magazine,* August 1934, p. 79.
Art of the Netherlands, Flanders and Holland, 15th-18th Centuries, at The Hermitage, Leningrad, Moscow, 1955, p. 67.
Bazin, 1958, pp. 184, 249, no. 281, pl. 182.
H. Fechner, *Jacob van Ruisdael* (in Russian), Leningrad, 1958, p. 17.
Hermitage Catalogue, 1958, II, p. 250, no. 934.
Descargues, 1961, pp. 140-141.
Levinson-Lessing, 1962, no. 48.
H. Fechner, *Dutch Landscapes of the Seventeenth Century in the Hermitage* (in Russian), Leningrad, 1963, pp. 70, 93-94, pls. 66-68.
Wolfgang Stechow, *Dutch Landscape Painting,* London, 1966, p. 75.
Jakob Rosenberg, Seymour Slive, E. H. ter Kuile, *Dutch Art and Architecture 1600-1800,* Baltimore, 1972, p. 268, pl. 214.
Kuznetsov, 1972, no. 50.

Thomas Gainsborough

English: Sudbury 1727 — London 1788

24. Portrait of a Lady late 1770's
Oil on canvas, 30⅛ x 25 in. (76.5 x 63.4 cm.)

At the age of thirteen Gainsborough left his native Suffolk for London, where he became a pupil of Hubert Gravelot (1699-1773). Returning to Suffolk in 1748, Gainsborough settled in Ipswich where he painted landscapes inspired by seventeenth century Dutch artists such as Hobbema and Ruisdael, and also gradually developed a personal style of portraiture. He moved to Bath in 1759 and received numerous portrait commissions there. In 1774 Gainsborough transferred his activity to London. His first royal commission, received in 1777, firmly established his reputation in the capital.

In the 1780's Gainsborough, in addition to his portraits and landscapes, began to paint "fancy pictures," sentimental genre scenes inspired by Murillo. In 1783 he quarreled with the Royal Academy, of which he was a founding member, over the hanging of his pictures and refused to exhibit there again. He nevertheless received the posthumous honor of being the only contemporary artist to be the subject of one of the *Discourses* by his great rival, Sir Joshua Reynolds, the President of the Academy.

Gainsborough's early portraits reveal his debt to the rococo manner of Gravelot and Francis Hayman. Later he turned to the more traditional and elegant portrait types of Van Dyck. Gainsborough concentrated on capturing the mood rather than the exact likeness of a sitter. In this respect and in his sketchy manner he is closer to French artists like Fragonard than to any English portraitists.

The Hermitage *Portrait of a Lady* is a characteristic example of Gainsborough's virtuoso technique which made him the most sought after painter of pretty women in late eighteenth century England. Different textures are suggested by subtly contrasted paint qualities. The diaphanous white dress is rendered so transparently that the sitter's skin shows through, while the wrap is painted more richly to convey the sheen of the silk. The lovely face, with its porcelain finish, looks ahead to Renoir. Gainsborough has employed a dark, resonant background to set off the pale tones of the flesh, the fragility of which is further accentuated by the blue of the wrap and hat ribbon and the black neck band. Here we see Van Dyck's portrait formula carried to an extreme of elegant refinement.

Without documentary evidence it is difficult to identify Gainsborough's sitters, especially the women. A. Z. Khitrovo, the collector who bequeathed this painting to the Hermitage, claimed that it represented the Duchess of Beaufort, presumably Elizabeth, wife of Henry, fifth Duke of Beaufort. This identification, however, has not been confirmed.

D.L.

Provenance:
Charles Wertheimer, London (?)
A. Z. Khitrovo, St. Petersburg, *ca.* 1892
Bequest of A. Z. Khitrovo to
The Hermitage, 1916

References:
Sir Walter Armstrong, *Gainsborough and His Place in English Art,* London and New York, 1899, p. 198.
Sir Walter Armstrong, *Gainsborough and His Place in English Art,* London and New York, 1904, p. 271.
Pierre P. Weiner, "The Collection of the late A. Z. Khitrovo at St. Petersburg," (in Russian) *Starye Gody,* December 1912, pp. 22, 23.
Weiner, 1923, pp. 310, 320.
Sir Martin Conway, *Art Treasures in Soviet Russia,* London, 1925, p. 168.
A. E. Kroll, "Exhibition of Portraits," (in Russian) *Iskusstvo,* 1938, no. 4, p. 42.
A. E. Kroll, *English Portraits of the 18th Century,* (in Russian) Leningrad, 1939, frontispiece and p. 45.
George Mihan, "Masterpieces Collected for the Hermitage by Catherine II and Her Successors," *Apollo,* April 1944, p. 111.
Ellis K. Waterhouse, "Preliminary Checklist of Portraits by Thomas Gainsborough," *Walpole Society,* XXXIII, 1953, p. 120, no. 8.
Bazin, 1958, pl. 201 and p. 194.
Hermitage Catalogue, 1958, II, p. 375, no. 3509 and p. 376, fig. 351.
Ellis K. Waterhouse, *Gainsborough,* London, 1958, p. 101, no. 792.
Descargues, 1961, p. 290.
A. E. Kroll, *English Painting of the XVIth-XIXth Centuries at the Hermitage Museum,* (in Russian) Leningrad, 1961, pp. 14, 81, 85 and pls. 26, 27, 28.
Levinson-Lessing, 1965, p. 92.
N. A. Livshits, *Art of the 18th Century; Historical Essays,* (in Russian) Moscow, 1966, p. 443.
Ellis K. Waterhouse, *Gainsborough,* London, 1966, p. 101, no. 792.
Kuznetsov, 1972, no 70.
Novoselskaya, 1972, pl. 38.

Exhibition:
Exhibition of Portraits XVIIIth-XXth Centuries, (in Russian) The Hermitage, Leningrad, 1938, part IV, no. 213.

Paul Cézanne

French: Aix-en-Provence 1839 — Aix-en-Provence 1906

25. Still Life *ca.* 1899
Oil on canvas, 21½ x 29⅛ in. (54.7 x 74 cm.)

In 1886 Cézanne's father, a Provençal banker, died leaving a substantial fortune. The artist, whose work had been repeatedly rejected by the *Salon* and mocked by critics and public alike, could now retire to the family's handsome house on the outskirts of Aix-en-Provence and devote himself to painting how and what he liked: the arid beauty of the Provençal scene, portraits of his wife and other models patient enough to put up with hundreds of sittings, groups of bathers who had of necessity to be done from imagination, and still lifes, frequently of wax fruit and paper flowers which were not subject, like the real thing, to change.

The exact dating of this still life and three related paintings (Venturi, Nos. 732, 742, and 745) presents a problem. Venturi dates this work *ca.* 1895, but John Rewald and Lawrence Gowing prefer 1899. Gowing furthermore believes, on the evidence of the floral drapery—a feature of all four still lifes, as well as *Mardi Gras* (Pushkin Museum, Moscow), which is known to have been painted in Paris—that this group was executed in Paris; however, this curtain may well have travelled back to Aix with the artist. Besides the drapery, each still life includes the same objects set on a plain wooden table: a jug decorated with flowers, and apples and oranges either on dishes, or strategically placed in the folds of white napkins.

At first sight the present picture (and Venturi No. 745, which is akin to it in organization) seems a relatively straightforward representation of a classic still life subject, but on closer examination anomalies emerge. The central dish of fruit, for instance, is tilted so precariously that it threatens to slide out at the onlooker. Likewise the tabletop slopes leftwards out of the picture, and the perspective of the side of the table is awry. Sometimes we seem to be looking up, sometimes down at objects, as if the artist had changed his viewpoint. There is nothing arbitrary in the liberties that Cézanne has taken. On the contrary, by subtly adjusting the way things look and registering tonal relationships with almost scientific precision, he has endowed his still life with an extra measure of tangible reality and heightened our experience of forms in space. In the other two more elaborate variants of this theme (Venturi Nos. 732 and 742), painted in the last years of his life, Cézanne switches his viewpoint even more drastically, in a way that anticipates cubist still lifes of 1908-09.

Far from being at odds with the rest of this highly worked picture, the "unfinished" passage in the right-hand bottom corner plays an important pictorial role. The transparency of this napkin provides a necessary note of spontaneity and emphasizes the solidity of everything else in the still life. It is also important to remember that Cézanne never thought in terms of "finished" pictures; he had the courage to stop before killing a picture with a last fatal brushstroke.

J.R.

Provenance:
A. Vollard, Paris
Ivan Morozov, Moscow, 1907
State Museum of Modern Western Art,
  Moscow, 1918
The Hermitage, 1930

References:
S. Makovsky, "French Artists of the I. A.
  Morozov Collection," (in Russian), *Apollon*,
  1912, no. 3, 4, pp. 28, 29.
Ambroise Vollard, *Paul Cézanne*, Paris, 1914,
  pl. 48.
Ternovietz, "Le Musée d'Art Moderne de Moscou
  (anciennes collections Stchoukine et Moro-
  soff)," *L'Amour de l'Art*, December 1925,
  p. 470.
Emile Bernard, *Souvenirs sur Paul Cézanne*,
  Paris, 1926, facing p. 92.
Howard Barnes, "Museums of Modern Art in
  Moscow," *The Arts*, August, 1927, p. 105.
*Musée d'Art Moderne de Moscou: Catalogue
  illustré*, Moscow, 1928, no. 561, p. 98, pl. 26.
Réau, 1929, no. 743, p. 100.
Lionello Venturi, *Cézanne, son art—son oeuvre*,
  Paris, 1936, I, no. 731, p.223, II, pl. 241.
"L'Art moderne français dans les collections des
  musées étrangers: Musée d'Art Moderne
  Occidental à Moscou," *Cahiers d'Art*, II,
  1950, no. 17, p. 338.
Lawrence Gowing, *An Exhibition of Paintings
  by Cézanne*, Edinburgh, Royal Scottish
  Academy, 1954, no. 58.
Hermitage Catalogue, 1958, I, no. 6514, p. 444,
  fig. 362.
Sterling, 1958, no. 32, p. 216.
Descargues, 1961, p. 299.
L. Voronikhina, *Art Treasures of the Hermitage*,
  Leningrad, 1961, pp. 162, 164.
Peter H. Feist, *Paul Cézanne*, Leipzig, 1963,
  no. 72.
Kuznetsov, 1967, no. 93.
Izergina *et al*, 1968, no. 56.
Ian Dunlop and Sandra Orienti, *The Complete
  Paintings of Cézanne*, New York, 1972,
  no. 794, pp. 122, 123.
Kuznetsov, 1972, no. 87.

Exhibitions:
French Art, XIIth to XXth Centuries,
  Hermitage, Leningrad, 1956.
Paul Cézanne, Hermitage, Leningrad, 1956,
  no. 22.
*One Hundred Masterpieces from USSR
  Museums*, Tokyo and Kyoto, 1971, no. 54.
From van Gogh to Picasso, State Museum
  Kröller-Müller, Otterlo, 1972, no. 4.
Impressionist Painting, Hermitage, Leningrad,
  1974.
*French Painting from the second half of the
  nineteenth to the beginning of the twentieth
  century*, Hermitage, Leningrad, 1975, no. 43.

Paul Gauguin

French: Paris 1848 — Atuana 1903

26. Where are you going? Où vas-tu? Ea Haere Ia Oe (II) 1893
Oil on canvas, 36¼ x 28¾ in. (92 x 73 cm.)
Signed and dated with title lower left: *P. Gauguin 93 Ea haere ia oe—*

Towards the end of his first visit to Tahiti Gauguin painted two versions of this composition. The earlier of these (Staatsgalerie, Stuttgart), dated 1892, differs from the Hermitage picture in that the girl is less nubile, more plainly dressed in an unpatterned *pareu,* and holds a small dog, instead of a breadfruit; also it does not have the woman carrying a child on the right. The artist had an evident fondness for the image of the crouching girl with the white blouse in the background of both compositions, as she is the main protagonist of the masterly *Quand te maries-tu?* (Kunstmuseum, Basel) of the previous year, and appears in two other compositions (Wildenstein, Nos. 445 and 477) and an important squared drawing in the Art Institute, Chicago. This crouching girl probably represents Gauguin's *vahiné,* Tehura, to judge by other paintings which are known to portray this beauty: *e.g. Queen of the Areois* (Mr. and Mrs. William Paley coll., New York). The principal figure of *Où vas-tu?* is more mature looking than Tehura, who would have been around fifteen at this time and pregnant.

Despite the '*93*' after the artist's signature, this picture is difficult to date with any exactitude. The likelihood is that Gauguin began it in 1892 and finished it sometime before May, 1893, when at his own request he was repatriated to France. However, according to John Rewald, Gauguin post-dated his *Pastorales Tahitiennes* (Hermitage), that is to say he inscribed it 1893, although it was actually completed in 1892; so he may well have done the same in the case of other pictures executed in 1892. Certainly Gauguin had good reason to put 1892—a year of declining health and desperate poverty—behind him. Since his eyesight failed between February and April, it is also possible that he finished the picture after his return to France in August, 1893, with sixty-six Tahitian paintings in his baggage but only four francs in his pocket.

Considering the miseries of his first Tahitian visit, Gauguin's paintings of the period are amazingly serene, even idyllic in mood. As Gauguin later wrote of these pictures and the village, Mataïea, some 25 kilometers from Papeete, where they were painted: "... I want to suggest an exuberant and wild nature and a tropical sun which sets on fire everything around it, I have to give my figures an appropriate frame. It really is open-air life, although intimate; in the thickets and the shaded brooks, those whispering women in an immense palace decorated by nature itself with all the riches that Tahiti holds. Hence these fabulous colors and this fiery yet softened and silent air."

According to L.-J. Bonge, once Governor of Tahiti, *Ea Haere Ia Oe* is a string of Tahitian syllables without meaning. *E Haera oi I hia* would mean "where are you going?"

J.R.

Provenance:
A. Vollard, Paris
Ivan Morozov, Moscow, 1908
State Museum of Modern Western Art, Moscow, 1918
The Hermitage, 1948

References:
S. Makovsky, "French Artists of the I. A. Morozov Collection," (in Russian) *Apollon,* 1912, nos. 3-4, p. 20.
Y. Tugendhold, *Moscow, Museum of Modern Western Art,* Moscow, 1923, pp. 138-9.
Erich Wiese, *Paul Gauguin,* Sammlung Junge Kunst, Leipzig, 1923, pl. IX.
B. N. Ternovietz, "Le Musée d'Art Moderne de Moscou (anciennes collections Stchoukine et Morosoff)" *L'Amour de l'Art,* December 1925, p. 472.
Catalogue of the State Museum of Modern Western Art, Moscow, 1928, no. 109, p. 34.
Réau, 1929, no. 851, p. 109.
Ternovetz, *Moscow, Museum of Modern Western Painting,* Moscow, 1935, p. XXI.
"L'Art moderne français dans les musées étrangers: Musée d'Art Moderne Occidental à Moscou," *Cahiers d'Art,* II, 1950, no. 109, p. 341.
Lee van Dovski, *Paul Gauguin,* Zurich, 1950, no. 265, p. 348.
Hermitage Catalogue, 1958, I, no. 9120, p. 371, pl. 292.
Sterling, 1958, p. 130, p. 136, no. 104.
Georges Wildenstein (ed.), *Gauguin, sa vie, son oeuvre,* Paris, 1958, p. 161.
Descargues, 1961, pp. 297, 308.
L. Voronikhina, *Art Treasures of the Hermitage,* Leningrad, 1961, pp. 163, 166.
Prokofiev, 1962, no. 155, p. 28.
Alfred Langer, *Paul Gauguin,* Leipzig, 1963, p. 48, p. 89, no. 49.
Georges Boudaille, *Gauguin,* London, 1964, p. 171.
Georges Wildenstein, *Gauguin,* Paris, 1964, I, no. 501, pp. 203-204.
A. S. Kantor-Gukovskaia, *Paul Gauguin,* Moscow, 1965, p. 116.
F. Cachin, *Gauguin,* Paris, 1968, p. 363.
Izergina *et al.,* 1968, no. 74.
John Bowlt, "Neo-Primitivism and Russian Painting," *The Burlington Magazine,* March 1974, p. 132, fig. 15, p. 137.

Exhibitions:
Gauguin, State Museum of Modern Western Art, Moscow, 1926, no. 11.
French Art, XIIth to XXth Centuries, Hermitage, Leningrad, 1956.
French Masters, Szepmuveszeti Museum, Budapest, 1969, no. 11.
Impressionist Painting, Hermitage, Leningrad, 1974, no. 7.

91

Henri Matisse

French: Le Cateau-Cambrésis 1869 — Nice 1954

27. Still Life with "The Dance" (Nature Morte à "La Danse") 1909
Oil on canvas, 35⅛ x 45⅞ in. (89.4 x 116.4 cm.)
Signed and dated lower right: *Henri Matisse 1909*

One of the most original colorists in the history of art and indisputably the greatest French artist of this century, Matisse devoted a lifetime to perfecting what he called "an art of balance, of purity and serenity . . ."

Son of a grain merchant in Picardy, Matisse first decided on a legal career and received his degree in 1888, but thanks to his mother's gift of a paint-box, he came to regret his choice and enrolled at a local art school. In 1891, he moved to Paris to study under the academic painter Bouguereau, at the *Académie Julian,* and take courses at the *Ecole des Arts Décoratifs.* Disappointed by Bouguereau's superficiality, Matisse moved on to Gustave Moreau's more progressive studio, where Rouault was already a student. Marquet, Manguin, Camoin—future *Fauves*—soon joined them. Early works include the usual copies after old masters in the Louvre, but the artist soon gravitated towards the Impressionists displayed in the Luxembourg. In 1898, on Pissarro's advice, Matisse went to London to study Turner's paintings. They did not impress him. Pissarro's advice was more to the point, when he warned Matisse against Symbolists and scientists, and showed him how to lighten his palette and experiment with textural effects.

The works of other artists—Gauguin, Rodin, Redon, Cézanne—which Matisse now acquired are a key to his preoccupations around the turn of the century. His Cézanne *Bathers* influenced him the most; it showed him how to animate space and build up form in terms of colored planes.

Matisse spent the next few years struggling to forge a strong new style based on Cézanne's discoveries. The breakthrough came in 1904, when he spent the summer at St.-Tropez working with Signac and Cross. At first Matisse resisted their attempts to convert him to the doctrine of Pointillism, but he finally succumbed and painted a large pointillist figure composition, *Luxe, Calme et Volupté.* His pointillist phase did not last long, but the experience was a profitable one. During the following summer (1905), spent with Derain at Collioure, Matisse succeeded in reconciling the influence of his new friends with that of Cézanne. The pictures that Matisse sent to the 1905 *Salon d'Automne,* where he and his colleagues were derisively labeled the *Fauves* (wild beasts), are triumphant proof of this new synthesis. Despite the public outcry, Matisse's most scandalous picture, *Woman with a Hat*—a portrait of his wife—was bought by Leo Stein, who with his brother and sister, Michael and Gertrude, became the artist's first patrons. Shortly afterwards, the Russian merchant, Sergei Shchukin, started acquiring many of Matisse's best works; by 1914, he owned thirty-seven paintings.

In March, 1909, Shchukin commissioned Matisse to paint two panels, *La Musique* and *La Danse* (both Hermitage) for the stairwell of his Moscow house, the eighteenth century Troubetzkoy Palace on Znamensky Lane. *La Danse* was finished in time to be exhibited alongside its pendant at the *Salon d'Automne* of 1910. Hung very high, they were an instant *succès de*

Provenance:
Bernheim Jeune & Cie., Paris,
Ivan Morozov, Moscow
State Museum of Modern Western Art,
  Moscow, 1918
The Hermitage, 1948

References:
S. Makovsky, "French Artists of the
  I. A. Morozov Collection," (in Russian),
  Apollon, no. 3-4, 1912, bet. pp. 48-49.
Ternovetz, "Le Musée d'Art Moderne de
  Moscou (anciennes collections Stchoukine
  et Morosoff)," *L'Amour de l'Art,* December
  1925, p. 484.
*Musée d'Art Moderne de Moscou: Catalogue
  illustré,* Moscow, 1928, p. 69, no. 351.
Réau, 1929, p. 119, no. 963.
"L'Oeuvre de Henri-Matisse," *Cahiers d'Art,*
  1931, no. 5-6, fig. 33.
Roger Fry, *Henri-Matisse,* New York, 1935,
  pl. 14.
"L'Art moderne français dans les collections
  des musées étrangers: Musée d'Art Moderne
  Occidental à Moscou," *Cahiers d'Art,* II,
  1950, p. 343, no. 46.
Alfred H. Barr, Jr., *Matisse, His Art and His
  Public,* New York, 1951, pp. 23, 104, 107,
  127, 128, 156, 346.
G. F. Hartlaub, *Matisse,* Wiesbaden, 1955, p. 8.
Hermitage Catalogue, 1958, I, p. 414, no. 9042.
Georges Charbonnier, "Entretien avec Henri
  Matisse," *Le Monologue du Peintre,* Paris,
  1960, II, pp. 7-16.
Gaston Diehl, *Henri Matisse,* Paris, 1970, p. 58.
Novoselskaya, 1972, pl. 54.
Albert Kostenevich, " 'La Danse' and 'La
  Musique' by Henri Matisse, A New
  Interpretation," *Apollo,* December 1974,
  p. 511, fig. 8 and p. 509.

Exhibitions:
Exposition Henri Matisse, Bernheim Jeune &
  Cie., Paris, 1910, no. 55.
Matisse, Moscow and Leningrad, 1969, no. 26.
Henri Matisse, exposition du centenaire, Grand
  Palais, Paris, 1970, no. 98.

Henri Matisse

scandale. Although Matisse had deliberately refrained from being too specific about the sex of his monumental nudes, Shchukin rejected the panels, on the grounds that they would shock his Russian friends, not to mention his two adopted daughters. After remonstrations from Matisse, the pictures were eventually accepted, although one rather explicit passage was repainted in Russia.

In order to have space in which to work on these vast canvases Matisse built a prefabricated wooden studio onto the house he had recently purchased in the Parisian suburb of Issy-les-Moulineaux, and paid for it out of the money that Shchukin had advanced him. This new studio is the setting for a carefully posed photograph of the artist at work on this very still life. This photograph (fig. 17), taken in the fall of 1909, is significant because it proves that the painting within this painting is not the definitive version of *La Danse* in the Hermitage, but the large sketch (fig. 18) for it in the Museum of Modern Art, New York. It further proves that Matisse did not paint this still life after he had finished the Museum of Modern Art's sketch. As the photograph reveals, both paintings are only blocked in, so the artist must have worked on the two compositions simultaneously. Whether Matisse had already begun to paint the big panels as well is uncertain, since the top right-hand corner of this still life and the photograph show the back of the stretcher and not the front of one of these very large canvases.

This still life thus serves as a running commentary on a major work in progress; it is a painting about the process of painting. Studio subjects which involve a measure of homage to his own art are a recurrent feature of Matisse's work, *e.g.* the two great mural compositions, *Les Capucines à la Danse* (Pushkin Museum, Moscow, and Worcester Art Museum, Massachusetts) painted in 1911, which establish an even closer rhythmic rapport than the present composition does between a floral still life and the Dionysiac figures of *La Danse*. Note also a series of intriguing works, *ca.* 1935, which show the hand of the artist making a drawing within a drawing of a scene that sometimes includes a self-portrait *(e.g.* Barr, p. 250).

The shrill colors and bold patterning that enliven this composition are largely a consequence of Matisse's visit to Biskra in North Africa in 1906. Arab crafts and textiles had opened the artist's eye to a whole new gamut of colors. At the same time he had developed a passion for decoration and arabesque—a passion that was confirmed in 1910 by his visit to the Islamic exhibition in Munich.

Matisse informed Georges Charbonnier that his inspiration for *La Danse* came one Sunday afternoon while he was watching the dancers at the popular musical hall, *Le Moulin de la Galette:* "Above all I watched the *farandole*. This *farandole* was very gay. Hand-in-hand, the dancers run across the room and grab hold of any bystanders . . . All this to a swinging tune . . . Back home as I worked on my dance I hummed the tune I had heard at the *Moulin de la Galette* to such good effect that the whole composition and the dancers are all together and dance to the same rhythm . . . It was in me this dance. I did not need any heating."

J.R.

fig. 17. Matisse in his studio at Issy-les-Moulineaux autumn, 1909, Courtesy Pierre Matisse.

fig. 18. Matisse, *La Danse,* oil, 9′ x 12′, Museum of Modern Art, New York.

Henri Matisse

28. The Painter's Family 1911
Oil on canvas, 58⅝ x 78⅜ in. (149 x 199 cm.)
Signed on the crossbar of the stretcher: *Henri Matisse 1911*

In 1911 Matisse painted four great interiors—Alfred Barr has called them "symphonic"—which are among his finest achievements. Three of these —*The Painter's Studio* (Pushkin Museum, Moscow), *Interior with Eggplants* (Musée de Peinture et de Sculpture, Grenoble), and *Red Studio* (Museum of Modern Art, New York)—are studio scenes in which pieces of sculpture and figure paintings are surrogates for people. The fourth, the Hermitage picture, is set in the artist's living room and includes "real" as opposed to "painted" figures. Of the four it is the most elaborate, not least because of the juxtaposition of highly patterned surfaces.

Matisse was a student of the decorative arts in his early years. More significant, in terms not only of this painting but of his future development, was his visit in 1910 to the important exhibition of Islamic art in Munich. The ornate rugs, textiles, tiles, metal work and Persian miniatures, which he studied on this occasion, transformed his vision. Matisse saw how decoration, hitherto often dismissed as a superficial adjunct, could play a crucial part in the harmonious organization of a composition and could enhance its "expression." "It is not pejorative," Matisse insisted to Léon Degand, "to say that the paintings of an artist are decorative. All our French primitives are decorative."

Decorative *The Painter's Family* certainly is, but it is also as grave and serene as the Le Nain (No. 8). Like Le Nain's figures, the members of the Matisse family, even the two sons playing checkers, are curiously remote from one another. Jack D. Flam has drawn attention to the "isolation and alienation" in Matisse's work in general and "the undercurrent of estrangement" in this picture.

Alfred Barr has published two postcards which Matisse wrote in the spring of 1911 to Michael Stein in San Francisco. The first one (dated May 26) states that this painting is unfinished, but "well under way . . . I am uncertain of its success." The second postcard is more specific: "The picture represents the living room with the fireplace in the middle and two couches on each side. On the couch at the left my wife works at her embroidery. In the middle Pierre and Jean are playing checkers and at the right Marguerite [the artist's daughter] is standing holding a yellow-bound book in her hand. She is in a black dress with white collar and white cuffs. The color is beautiful and generous."

Barr relates the subject of this picture to Matisse's monumental *Conversation* (Pushkin Museum, Moscow) painted two years earlier, but it has a more striking precedent in the simplifications of *The Game of Bowls* (Hermitage) of 1908—simplifications which, according to Picasso, were influenced by the childish drawings which Matisse's two sons had been doing.

J.R.

Provenance:
The artist, from whom it was acquired by Sergei Shchukin, Moscow
State Museum of Modern Western Art, Moscow, 1918
The Hermitage, 1948

References:
Y. Tugendhold, "Shchukin's Collection of French Painting, (in Russian) *Apollon*, 1914, no 1, 2, pp. 41, 57.
Ternovetz, "Le Musée d'Art Moderne de Moscou (anciennes collections Stchoukine et Morosoff)," *L'Amour de l'Art*, December 1925, p. 484.
Paul Ettinger, "Die modernen Franzosen in den Kunstsammlungen Moskaus—Part II," *Der Cicerone*, 1926, no. 4, pp. 112, 119.
Howard Barnes, "Museums of Modern Art in Moscow," *The Arts*, August 1927, p. 104.
Musée d'Art Moderne de Moscou: Catalogue illustré, Moscow, 1928, p. 65, no. 319, pl. 13.
Réau, 1929, p. 117, no. 930.
B. N. Ternovetz, *Museum of Western Art, Moscow: Portfolio Number One*, Moscow, n.d. (1937?), pl. 23.
Raymond Escholier, *Henri Matisse*, Paris, 1937, bet. pp. 38-43.
Léon Degand, "Matisse à Paris," *Les Lettres Françaises*, no. 76, October 6, 1945.
"L'Art moderne français dans les collections des musées étrangers: Musée d'Art Moderne Occidental à Moscou," *Cahiers d'Art*, II, 1950, p. 343, no. 14.
Alfred H. Barr, Jr., *Matisse, His Art and His Public*, New York, 1951, pp. 28, 42, 143, 151, 152, 153, 157, 193, 211, 269, 373.
Gaston Diehl, *Henri Matisse*, Paris, 1954, pp. 61, 62, 154.
Hermitage Catalogue, 1958, I, p. 414, no. 8940, p. 409, fig. 327.
Sterling, 1958, p. 178 and p. 187, no. 143.
André Chastel, "Leningrad: French Masters of The Hermitage," *Art News*, April 1958, p. 37.
John Russell, "Notes from Europe—Sightseeing in Russian Museums," *Art in America*, Fall 1958, p. 87.
Jacques Lassaigne, *Matisse*, Geneva, 1959, pp. 67, 69.
Descargues, 1961, p. 304.
Gaston Diehl, *Henri Matisse*, Paris, 1970, p. 59.
Izergina *et al.*, 1970, pl. 30, 31.
Kuznetsov, 1972, no. 97.
Jack D. Flam, "Some Observations on Matisse's Self-Portraits," *Arts*, May 1975, p. 51.

Exhibitions:
Matisse, Moscow and Leningrad, 1969, no. 35.

Pablo Ruiz Picasso

Spanish: Malaga 1881 — Mougins 1973

29. Friendship (L'Amitié) 1908
Oil on canvas, 59¼ x 39½ in. (150.5 x 100.5 cm.)
Signed on the back: *Picasso*

Picasso's formative years were spent in Barcelona, the most progressive and independent city in Spain, also a hotbed of *art nouveau* activity, but he soon outshone the rest of the Catalan artists. Finding Barcelona confining, he set off in 1900 for Paris; where he acquainted himself with recent developments in French art. Steinlen, Toulouse-Lautrec, van Gogh, Gauguin, the *Nabis,* each had something to offer him. He also devoured all he saw in the Louvre. This artistic gorging resulted in a succession of violent oscillations in style and subject. The changes in subject matter—colorful *demi-monde* scenes give way to low life—reflect changes in the artist's attitude as well as circumstances. "All that was just sentiment:" Picasso's later dismissal of his Blue Period is apt, but the best of these early works transcend self-pity.

By 1906 blue had given way to pink, and Spanish gloom to Parisian sentiment, but Picasso was too much of a rebel to be satisfied with the charms of his so-called Pink Period. In the summer of 1906 he went off to the Pyrenees to forge a tougher, simpler style, based on primitive Iberian sculpture. Back in Paris, he worked out his new ideas in a large figure composition, *Les Demoiselles d'Avignon* (Museum of Modern Art, New York) of 1907. Here at last was the synthesis towards which he had been feeling his way. Iberian sculpture, African art, Cézanne and other influences had been fused into a style that was personal, revolutionary and expressive.

In 1907, Picasso met Braque, and for the next seven years the two artists devoted themselves to developing the style known as Cubism. The most influential art movement of the twentieth century, Cubism was never an artistic theory or method, or a magic picture-making formula, but a new pictorial means of representing form and space. Cubism was constantly subject to modification, because its two creators were intuitive, as opposed to scientific, in their approach. All they had to guide them were the pioneer discoveries of Cézanne, and these they soon outstripped.

One of Picasso's few traditional traits was a tendency, at least in his early days, to envisage his work in terms of ambitious *chefs-d'oeuvre* which would sum up his latest stylistic developments and establish his leadership of the *avant garde*. For months Picasso would circle the subject he had in mind, sometimes achieving a major breakthrough, as with *Les Demoiselles d'Avignon,* and at other times becoming so absorbed in the preparatory studies that the definitive composition never saw the light of day (*e.g.* the two great compositions of circus people that he planned in 1905, of which only one, *Les Saltimbanques,* National Gallery, Washington, was executed). Given the quality and variety of the preliminary work and the fact that the artist was always most successful with tightly organized compositions, the absence of these setpieces is not necessarily to be regretted.

Despite its revolutionary innovations, the *Demoiselles* is stylistically

Provenance:
Galerie Kahnweiler, Paris
Sergei Shchukin, Moscow
State Museum of Modern Western Art,
    Moscow, 1918
The Hermitage, 1931

References:
G. Chulkov, "Demons and the World Today,"
    (in Russian) *Apollon,* nos. 1-2, 1914, p. 74.
Y. Tugendhold, "Shchukin's Collection of
    French Painting," (in Russian) *Apollon,*
    nos. 1-2, 1914, p. 44.
*Musée d'art moderne de Moscou: Catalogue
    illustré,* Moscow, 1928, p. 81, no. 431.
Réau, 1929, p. 124, no. 1019.
Eugenio d'Ors, *Pablo Picasso,* Paris and New
    York, 1930, pl. 15 and no. 15.
Christian Zervos, *Pablo Picasso,* II,[*] Paris, 1942,
    no. 60 and pl. 31.
Alfred H. Barr, Jr., *Picasso. Fifty Years of
    His Art,* New York, 1946, p. 61.
Joan Merli, *Picasso,* Buenos Aires, 1948, fig. 170
    and p. 600, no. 170.
"L'Art moderne français dans les collections
    des musées étrangers: Musée d'Art Moderne
    Occidental à Moscou," *Cahiers d'Art,*
    II, 1950, p. 345, no. 431.
Frank Elgar and Robert Maillard, *Picasso,* Paris,
    1955, p. 304.
Vercors, *Picasso. Oeuvres des musées de
    Leningrad et de Moscou. et de quelques
    collections parisiennes,* Paris, 1955, p. 85,
    no. 31.
José Camón Aznar, *Picasso y el Cubismo,*
    Madrid, 1956, p. 389, fig. 281.
Hermitage Catalogue, 1958, I, p. 427, no. 6576.
Roland Penrose, *Picasso: His Life and Work,*
    London, 1958, pl. V, fig. 6 and pp. 132, 133.
Izergina *et al.,* 1970, no. 71.

Exhibitions:
*Picasso. Oeuvres des musées de Leningrad et
    de Moscou. 1900-1914,* Maison de la Pensée
    Française, Paris, 1954, no. 8.
Picasso dans les musées soviétiques, Musée
    National d'Art Moderne, Paris, 1971, no. 8

Pablo Ruiz Picasso

unresolved—hence Picasso's need to embark on another major composition. He spent the winter of 1907-08 and the following spring making numerous studies (*e.g.* fig. 19) of groups of bathers, with draperies or towels, posing under trees beside a river. One composition involves a single figure, another two, another three and a fourth five figures, the last being an ambitious combination of the two other groups. Just as he had reduced the *Demoiselles* from seven to five figures, Picasso eliminated the five-figure idea and kept to the more compact configurations. He transformed the three bathers on the right of fig. 19, who seem to be drying themselves with towels, into the monumental *Les Trois Femmes* (Hermitage). And after many more studies (*e.g.* figs. 20 and 21) the two women with their arms around one another's necks, on the left of fig. 19, were worked up into this powerful composition.

Cézanne was Picasso's main inspiration. Through Vollard, the Paris dealer, Picasso had known Cézanne's work at first hand for at least six years, but it was not until the Cézanne Retrospective at the *Salon d'Automne* in 1906—an exhibition which changed the course of twentieth century art—that the influence of the Master of Aix began to permeate Picasso's work. Cézanne's revolutionary concept of volumes ("treat nature in terms of the cylinder, sphere and cone . . ."), his structural use of color, his no less structural brushwork, his taut way with compositions which seem to be built upon armatures, his subjects, all left their mark on Picasso. If this influence is not immediately evident, it is because the young Spaniard was clever at covering his tracks. Moreover, the liberties that Picasso takes with appearances are so much more radical than Cézanne's—a consequence of his simultaneous use of primitive elements borrowed from African art.

L'Amitié is thus a stylistic hybrid. The blank, mask-like faces and brutal simplifications stem from African sculpture. But the degree to which the volumes of the figures and the setting are organic parts of an organic whole, and the way the planes open up rhythmically into one another is essentially Cézannesque, as are the restrained earthy colors. *L'Amitié* reveals what a viable synthesis Picasso had been able to make out of two diametrically opposed sources—African art which is essentially conceptual and Cézanne's art which is essentially perceptual. This synthesis made Cubism possible for Picasso.

The artist was too involved in purely pictorial matters to have any abstract concepts of friendship in mind when he was at work on this composition, nor was he in the habit of baptizing his pictures, so no special significance should be attached to this title. "*L'Amitié*" was probably coined by the picture's first owner, Sergei Shchukin, whose progessive views on art did not preclude a certain prudishness. It would be in keeping with Shchukin's nature to disguise the equivocal subject of this picture with a euphemistic title.

J.R.

fig. 19. Picasso, *Bathers,* winter, 1907-08, watercolor, Museum of Modern Art, New York.
fig. 20. Picasso, Study for *Friendship,* winter, 1907-08, gouache, Pushkin Museum, Moscow.
fig. 21. Picasso, Study for *Friendship,* winter, 1907-08, gouache, Pushkin Museum, Moscow.

Pablo Ruiz Picasso

30. Woman with a Fan Summer, 1908
Oil on canvas, 59½ x 39⅝ in. (151 x 100.6 cm.)

The suicide of Picasso's friend, the German painter Vighels, in the summer of 1908 left the artist in a state of nervous torpor. Instead of going to Spain, as was his summer habit, he stayed for a few weeks on a farm in the village of Rue-des-Bois, on the edge of the Forêt d'Hallatte, near Creil. His intention was to relax, but he took a dislike to the countryside. Characteristically he threw himself into work and produced still lifes and landscapes, which recall Cézanne, and some figure paintings inspired by the stolid appearance of his landlady, Madame Putman. At Rue-des-Bois, or on his return to Paris, he also painted this *Woman with a Fan*. The rudimentary features resemble those in the paintings of Madame Putman, but the elegance of the figure does not accord with the landlady's peasant build. It is more likely that Picasso had his mistress, Fernande Olivier, in mind. A preparatory drawing (Zervos, Vol. II,** No. 700) for this painting is unmistakably of Fernande, although, like the *Woman With a Fan*, her nose has been replaced with a Cézannesque cone. Two other preparatory drawings (*ibid*. Nos. 701-02) show how this composition developed from a relatively representational conception, that recalls some of Cézanne's portraits of his wife, to this stylized image. A marked feature of these three drawings is the exaggeratedly uneven shoulders, which accentuate the diagonal axis of the body.

In *Woman with a Fan* the synthesis of African and Cézannesque elements has been carried a stage further than it was in *L'Amitié* (No. 29). The hieratic sculptural look of African art persists, but the self-conscious primitivism and violently striated brushstrokes have vanished. Meanwhile Picasso's debt to Cézanne has if anything increased, as witness the rhythms, rhyming forms and geometrical simplifications of this austere yet harmonious composition. And also, as John Golding has written (*Cubism*, 1959), "What seems to have fascinated Picasso about Cézanne's figure studies and portraits . . . is the complete disregard of details, which is at times extended even to the individual features of the face."

In Shchukin's catalogue of 1913 this painting is entitled *After the Ball;* as a result it has been hailed in Russia as a conscious challenge on the part of the artist to nineteenth century genre paintings with this insipid kind of theme. However, Picasso seldom named his pictures and would never have thought up such a title as this, even in irony or jest. That the sobriquet was yet another of Shchukin's inventions can be safely assumed. True, the fan could have a sexual significance, but its appeal to Picasso lay surely in the way that its articulated surface makes a perfect foil for the flat planes of the rest of the picture. Even more to the point, the summer of 1908 was exceedingly hot, hence conceivably the *décolletage* as well as the fan. Shchukin also owned another *Woman with Fan* (Pushkin Museum, Moscow)—his first Picasso—which dates from the following year. Once again a fan provides the artist with a useful pictorial device. The articulation of form was after all a major preoccupation of the Cubists.   J.R.

Provenance:
Galerie Kahnweiler, Paris
Sergei Shchukin, Moscow
State Museum of Modern Western Art,
   Moscow, 1918
The Hermitage, 1934

References:
G. Chulkov, "Demons and the World Today,"
   (in Russian) *Apollon*, nos. 1-2, 1914, p. 73.
Y. Tugendhold, "Shchukin's Collection of
   French Painting," (in Russian) *Apollon*,
   nos. 1-2, 1914, p. 43.
*Musée d'art moderne de Moscou: Catalogue
   illustré*, Moscow, 1928, p. 81, no. 436.
Réau, 1929, p. 125, no. 1024.
Christian Zervos, *Pablo Picasso*, II*, Paris, 1942,
   no. 67 and pl. 35.
"L'Art moderne français dans les collections des
   musées étrangers: Musée d'Art Moderne
   Occidental à Moscou," *Cahiers d'Art*, II, 1950,
   p. 345, no. 436.
Wilhelm Boeck and Jaimé Sarbartés, *Picasso*,
   New York and Amsterdam, 1955, p. 461,
   no. 40, and p. 148.
Frank Elgar and Robert Maillard, *Picasso*, Paris,
   1955, pp. 268, 304.
Vercors, *Picasso. Oeuvres des musées de
   Leningrad et de Moscou, et de quelques
   collections parisiennes*, Paris, 1955, p. 87.
   fig. 32, and no. 32.
Hermitage Catalogue, 1958, I, p. 427, no. 7705
   and fig. 345.
Hans L. C. Jaffé, *Pablo Picasso*, New York,
   1964, p. 83.
Kermit S. Champa, "Paris: From Russia with
   Love," *Arts Magazine*, September-October
   1965, p. 56.
P. M. Grand, "The Russian Delegation to Paris,"
   Art News, October 1965, p. 61.
Izergina *et al.*, 1970, no. 72.

Exhibitions:
*Picasso. Oeuvres des musées de Leningrad et de
   Moscou, 1900-1914*, Maison de la Pensée
   Française, Paris, 1954, no. 9.
French Art XIIth to XXth Centuries, The
   Hermitage, Leningrad, 1956, p. 47.
50 Ans d'art moderne, Palais International des
   Beaux-Arts, Brussels, 1958, no. 256.
*Chefs-d'oeuvre de la peinture française dans les
   Musées de Leningrad et de Moscou*, Bordeaux,
   1965, no. 93.
Hommage à Pablo Picasso, Grand Palais, Paris,
   1966-1967, no. 53.

Introduction

The Mikhailovsky Palace was built in the first quarter of the nineteenth century by the architect Carlo Rossi. Located on the Square of the Arts, it is one of the most attractive buildings in Leningrad and was opened as the first state museum of national art and culture in 1898. Apart from works of art, it included ethnographical and historical departments.

The basic collection consisted of paintings and sculpture from the Academy of Arts, Hermitage and other Royal palaces—the Winter Palace, Gatchina Palace and Tsar Alexander Village. The collection formed in this way was comparatively small and not very systematically organized. Works by Russian artists of the eighteenth and first half of the nineteenth centuries predominated because of the artistic bonds that linked these masters with the Academy of Arts. The more recent epochs in the history of Russian Art were also represented, but by relatively few works, most of them by painters of the academic school.

Over the years the number of exhibits increased, as several valuable private collections were acquired, but until 1917 the museum remained incomplete, and the exhibits were displayed in galleries without any definite scientific order. Nevertheless the opening of a museum which could boast a number of key works of the national school was a significant event in Russian cultural life of the period.

The October Revolution opened up new prospects of development for the museum and radically changed both its appearance and the nature of its activities. In the course of the first post-revolutionary years the holdings of the State Russian Museum increased several times over, thanks to the acquisition of collections of great artistic value from palaces, churches and noblemen's palaces. Among the works of art now shown to a wide audience were many unique paintings, such as the series of portraits of students from the Smolny Institute by the famous Russian portrait-painter, D. G. Levitsky. One painting (No. 31) out of this series is included in the present exhibition. Apart from painting, sculpture and drawings, the museum was enriched by the acquisition of items of folk art and the applied arts which had hitherto been virtually unrepresented in the museum.

In the early 1930's the art section became fully independent and was reorganized into the State Russian Museum, and it is now the largest repository of national art in the country. It includes a numerous and comprehensive collection of paintings, a collection of Russian sculpture unique in completeness and size, many thousands of objects of ancient Russian art, applied art and folk art, and vast collections of drawings and prints.

The thirteen paintings shown in the present exhibition are by the best known masters. Although it has not been possible to demonstrate the full range of the most famous painters of Russia, the selection gives an idea of the development of Russian art over one hundred and thirty years, beginning with the last quarter of the eighteenth century.

The greatest Russian painter of the first half of the nineteenth century and one of the first to tackle the problems of painting in the open air was A. A. Ivanov, whose works are exhibited in two rooms of the State Russian Museum. One of his landscape studies (No. 34) is included in this show. Another important painting is *A View of Constantinople* (No. 35), a characteristic work by I. R. Aivazovsky, the marine painter and master of romantic landscapes of the middle of the last century. The section devoted to the first half of the nineteenth century ends with a work (No. 32) by the founder of realistic genre painting in Russia, A. G. Venetsianov.

The second half of the nineteenth century saw the flowering of the democratic art of social realism which ultimately dominated Russian painting. This movement was based on the brilliant aesthetic ideas of a group of artists who banded themelves together in 1870 as the *Peredvizhniki,* "The Society for Traveling Exhibitions." This period of Russian art is represented in the present exhibition by the outstanding portraitist and leader of the Society, I. N. Kramskoy (No. 36); by the master of landscape painting, I. I. Levitan (No. 40); and by the great master of Russian realist painting of the last century, I. E. Repin (Nos. 38 and 39).

Russian artists of the twentieth century developed out of the best traditions of the masters of the previous generation. They introduced in their creative activity a new artistic expressiveness, graphic subtlety and stylistic variety. This brilliant period is well represented in the Museum's collections, and is reflected in three portraits by outstanding masters of Russian painting, V. A. Serov, L. S. Bakst and K. A. Somov in the present exhibition.

V. P. Pushkarev
Director of the State Russian Museum, Candidate of Arts

Paintings from The State Russian Museum

Commentaries:
Magdalena Dabrowski and
John Richardson

Provenances and Bibliographies:
Magdalena Dabrowski, based on
information supplied by the
State Russian Museum

Dimitri Grigorievich Levitsky

Kiev 1735 — St. Petersburg (?) 1822

31. Portrait of Catherine Nelidov 1773
Oil on canvas, 64½ x 41¾ in. (164 x 106 cm.)
Signed and dated center left: *P. D. Levitsky 1773*

Levitsky, one of the most prominent portrait painters of the time of Catherine the Great, came of Ukrainian stock. He received some early training from his father, a priest who was also a skilled engraver; but his first formal teacher was Alexei Antropov, who came to Kiev in 1752 to execute the decorations for the Cathedral of Saint Andrew. Levitsky probably helped in this work. When, in 1756, Antropov was recalled to Moscow he took his *protégé* with him. Subsequently (1769) Levitsky settled in St. Petersburg, where he studied at the Academy of Arts, possibly under the Frenchman, Louis-Jean-François Lagrenée, and the Venetian, Giuseppe Valeriani.

Levitsky's early paintings are strongly influenced by Tocqué and Michel van Loo, whose work he probably knew through Lagrenée. His portrait of the architect, Kokorinov, in the manner of Tocqué brought him favorable notice at the Academy exhibition of 1770. As a result he was invited to join the Academy as a professor of portraiture the following year. He held this position until his resignation in 1788; in the meantime (1776) he had been appointed one of the six members of the Academy Council. From 1780 onwards Levitsky was an official portraitist to the Russian court, executing a series of portraits of Catherine the Great. Following the creation of the Saint Vladimir Order of Knighthood by her in 1782, Levitsky was commissioned to paint portraits of the holders of the Great Cross for the hall of the Order. Towards the mid-1780's his style changed considerably; he abandoned his decorative, French-influenced manner for a somewhat simpler approach. After 1795 Levitsky developed a neo-classical style.

The *Portrait of Catherine Nelidov* commissioned by Catherine II is one of seven portraits of her favorite pupils at the Smolny Institute (the Imperial College for Daughters of the Nobility). Among Levitsky's finest works, they date from 1772-1776, and this portrait is among the earliest.

Catherine Nelidov, the future mistress of Tsar Paul I, was born in 1758. In 1776 she was named a lady-in-waiting, first to the Grand Duchess Nathalia Alekseevna, then, after the latter's death, to the Grand Duchess— and future Empress—Maria Fedorovna. In this almost life-size portrait Catherine Nelidov, who was renowned for her ability as a dancer, is represented performing a minuet, and wearing the fine taffeta dress customary for Smolny students on festive occasions.

In this free and animated composition full of rococo charm, Levitsky displays his skill at capturing the various textures and delicate detail of the girl's dress, as well as the vivacity of her personality.

Provenance:
Grand Palace, Peterhof
The State Russian Museum, Leningrad, 1917

References:
Mir Iskusstva, March-April 1899, p. 41.
Sergei Diaghilev, "D. G. Levitsky 1735-1822," *Russian Painting of the XVIIIth Century,* St. Petersburg, 1902, I, p. 49, pl. 19.
Denis Roche, "D. G. Levitsky," *Gazette des Beaux-Arts,* June 1903, p. 503-505.
Jean-José Frappa, "Un Grand peintre russe au XVIIIe siècle. Dimitri Levitsky," *Supplément d'Art de Je Sais Tout,* (deuxième année, serie VI), 1906, p. 715-722.
Louis Réau, *L'Art Russe,* Paris, 1922, II, pp. 125-128.
N. M. Chegodaeva, "D. G. Levitski," *Istoria russkavo iskusstva,* (edited by Igor Grabar and A. Fedorov-Davydov), 1961, VII, pp. 53-56.
N. Novouspensky, *Painting. The Russian Museum,* Leningrad, 1974, p. 6, pl. 13.

Additional Bibliography:
Denis Roche, "D. G. Levitsky," *Gazette des Beaux-Arts,* June 1903, pp. 494-507, October 1903, pp. 318-332.
A. Skvortsov, *D. G. Levitsky,* Moscow, 1916.
N. M. Gerschenson-Chegodaeva, *Dimitri Grigorievich Levitsky,* Moscow, 1964.
Richard Hare, *The Art and Artists of Russia,* London, 1965, pp. 119-120.
I. Ostroukhov, *D. G. Levitsky and V. S. Borovikovsky,* St. Petersburg, n.d.

Exhibitions:
Historical Exhibition of Portraiture XVIth-XVIIIth Centuries, St. Petersburg, 1870, no. 495.
150 Years of Russian Portraiture (1700-1850), St. Petersburg, 1902.
Exhibition of Russian Portraiture, Tauride Palace, St. Petersburg, 1905, no. 843.
Exposition de l'Art Russe, Salon d'Automne, Paris, 1906, no. 309.
Russische Kunst-Ausstellung, Berlin, 1906-1907, no. 256.
Russian Art from the XIIIth Century to the Present, National Museum, Warsaw, 1969.
One Hundred Masterpieces from USSR Museums, Tokyo and Kyoto, 1971, no. 76.
Portrait Painting in European Art, XVth— beginning of the XXth Century, Moscow, 1972.

Alexei Gavrilovich Venetsianov

Moscow 1780 — Safonkovo 1847

32. Fortune Telling, 1842
Oil on canvas, 28⅜ x 24⅝ in. (72.2 x 62.7 cm.)
Signed and dated lower left: *A. Venetsianov 1842 s. Safonk.*

Venetsianov was an important realist and the creator of the Russian genre of peasant painting. He remained in Moscow until his twenties, becoming interested in painting about 1800.

Early works were mainly portraits of members of his family, done in pastel or oil. After a few brief trips to St. Petersburg, he decided to move there around 1807, to work as a post office clerk, and paint in his free time. Soon after his arrival he met the portrait painter V. S. Borovikovsky and became his pupil. At the same time Venetsianov studied and copied the old masters in the Hermitage. He also worked as a caricaturist, and published *The Journal of Caricature* (1808). Here his style reveals the influence of Russian folk art, particularly the *loubok* (eighteenth and early nineteenth century peasant woodcuts). After three issues *The Journal* was banned by the censors because of its violently anti-bourgeois attitude. Venetsianov, however, took up caricature again during the Napoleonic war, making the French and their Emperor the target of his satire.

By 1811 Venetsianov's portraits had won him a place at the Academy, but eight years passed before he resigned his governmental post to devote his life to painting. In 1819 he settled at Safonkovo in the province of Tver (now Kalinin), where he formed his own art school. The move from urban St. Petersburg to the country led to a decisive change in Venetsianov's subject matter. For the remainder of his career he concentrated on painting portraits and genre scenes drawn from the life of the local peasantry.

In Venetsianov's late works his figures are relatively stylized, as in this painting of two buxom peasant girls from the village of Safonkovo, engaged in a popular pastime—reading their future in the cards. Typical of this artist is the expression of innocence on the girls' faces, as they wait for the cards to reveal their destinies. Unlike Venetsianov's earlier works in this genre which are more down-to-earth, these peasant girls have a nobility that hardly corresponds to their situation. The artist has transformed them into classical beauties that recall Raphael.

Venetsianov painted a replica of this painting, which originally was in the Popov collection, Moscow, and later belonged to S. S. Khroulev in St. Petersburg.

Provenance:
S. N. Galyashkin, Moscow
The Russian Museum of The Emperor
    Alexander III, 1898
The State Russian Museum, Leningrad

Bibliography:
Richard Muther, *History of Modern Painting,*
    London, 1907.
Alexandre Benois, *The Russian School of
    Painting,* New York, 1916, pp. 115-6.
N. Mashkovtsev, *A. G. Venetsianov,* Moscow,
    1944.
N. Dmitrieva, "A. G. Venetsianov," *Iskusstvo,*
    January-February, 1948.
Z. I. Fomicheva, *A. G. Venetsianov as a Teacher,*
    Moscow, 1952.
Mikhail V. Alpatov, *A. G. Venetsianov,*
    Moscow, 1954.
A. N. Savinov, *A. G. Venetsianov, His Life
    and Work,* Moscow, 1955.
T. Alekseeva, "Development of the Early Works
    of Venetsianov," *Ezhegodnik,* 1956,
    pp. 201-253.
Tretyakov Gallery, *Drawings and Watercolors:
    A. G. Venetsianov,* Moscow, 1956.
Mikhail V. Alpatov, *Wenezianov,* Dresden, 1962,
    I, pp. 305-321.
T. Alekseeva, "A. G. Venetsianov and the
    Development of Genre Painting," *History of
    Russian Art* (edited by Igor Grabar and
    A. Fedorov-Davydov), Moscow, 1965, VIII,
    pp. 546-598.
G. V. Smirnov (ed.), *Venetsianov and his
    School,* Leningrad, 1973.

Exhibitions:
Exhibition of Paintings, Imperial Academy of
    Fine Arts, St. Petersburg, 1852, no. 152.

Karl Ivanovich Briullov

St. Petersburg 1799 — Marciano 1852

33. Self-Portrait 1849
Oil on board, 26⅜ x 21¼ in. (67 x 54 cm.)

Briullov was one of the most important Russian painters of the first half of the nineteenth century. His career encompassed both the neo-classical and romantic movements. The son of an Italian carver who had settled in St. Petersburg, he entered the Academy at the age of ten, studying there under A. I. Ivanov. Having completed his training in 1822, Briullov went abroad, first to Rome, and for the next thirteen years, traveled extensively through Germany and Italy. In 1836 he returned to St. Petersburg and a professorship at the Academy of Arts. His poor health, however, forced him to leave Russia for good in 1849, and he visited Belgium, England, Madeira, and Spain. In the spring of 1850 he settled again in Italy and remained there until his death.

At the outset of Briullov's career, large-scale historical or religious compositions were the fashion; accordingly, he concentrated on popular classical and sentimental subjects with which he had considerable success in his native Russia. He also won international acclaim for his enormous *tour de force, The Last Days of Pompeii* (1828-1830, State Russian Museum, Leningrad), executed in an eclectic style derived from Raphael, Poussin, David, and Horace Vernet. Appropriately this fustian production provided Bulwer-Lytton with the subject of an equally popular epic novel with the same title.

Briullov was also much in demand for his portraits, particularly those of attractive women in fancy dress, on horseback, or in gardens. Briullov's portraits of men are less worldly and more penetrating, particularly his self-portraits. The most striking of these is the one dated 1848, in the Tretyakov Gallery, Moscow. The version exhibited here is a replica of it painted for Countess S. A. Bobrinskaya. According to the State Russian Museum, Briullov originally entrusted the execution of this version to one of his students, but later reworked it himself. Certainly the technical brilliance and intensely introspective air would seem to indicate that the major contribution is Briullov's.

This portrait represents the artist at a time when he was already suffering from serious physical and nervous illness, hence the pallor and self-pity, the weariness and disillusionment of the pose. Even the transparently painted, flaccid right hand hanging weakly over the edge of the chair conveys a sense of resignation. The refinement of this hand, indeed of the whole portrait, recalls the elegance of Van Dyck's early *Self-Portrait* in the Hermitage, which Briullov would surely have known.

Provenance:
Commissioned by Count A. A. Bobrinsky,
  ca. 1849
The Russian Museum of The Emperor
  Alexander III, St. Petersburg, 1898
The State Russian Museum, Leningrad

References:
Magdalina M. Rakova, *Briullov, Portrait Painter,*
  Moscow, 1956, pp. 127-131.
E. N. Atsarkina, "K. P. Briullov," in *History of
  Russian Painting,* Moscow, 1965, VIII, part 1,
  p. 92.

Additional Bibliography:
N. Wrangel, *Russian Museum of the Emperor
  Alexander III, Painting and Sculpture,*
  St. Petersburg, 1904, I.
Richard Muther, *The History of Modern
  Painting,* London, 1907, 4, pp. 243-246,
  249-251, 392.
D. Arkin and B. Ternovetz, *Masters of Art
  on Art,* Moscow, 1937, pp. 101-116.
N. Mashkovtsev, *K. P. Briullov in Letters,
  Documents, and Reminiscences of his
  Contemporaries,* Moscow, 1952.
George Heard Hamilton, *The Art and
  Architecture of Russia,* Baltimore, 1954,
  p. 238.
Mikhail V. Alpatov, *K. P. Briullov,* Moscow,
  1955.
*Drawings and Watercolors: K. P. Briullov and
  Others (Album),* Tretyakov Gallery, Moscow,
  1956.
Magdalina M. Rakova, *Briullov, Portrait Painter,*
  Moscow, 1956.
*State Russian Museum, Guidebook to the
  Collections,* Leningrad and Moscow, 1958.
E. N. Atsarkina, "K. P. Briullov," in *History of
  Russian Painting,* Moscow, 1965, VIII, part 1,
  pp. 43-109.

Aleksandr Andreyevich Ivanov

St. Petersburg 1806 — St. Petersburg 1858

34. Water and Rocks Near Palazzuola early 1850's
Oil on paper, 18⅜ x 25 in. (46.7 x 63.7 cm.)

Although originally a painter in the fashionable neo-classical idiom, Ivanov was to become a leader of the romantic movement and the first Russian artist to paint in the open air. His father taught history painting at the St. Petersburg Academy of Arts, where from 1817 to 1828 the young Ivanov received his training. After winning several awards for his classical and Biblical compositions, he was the recipient of a travel grant from the Society for the Encouragement of the Arts, which enabled him to go to Rome in 1830. He remained in Italy for nearly three decades, not returning to St. Petersburg until the year of his death. Ivanov's combination of a spiritual with a naturalistic approach was of great importance for the following generation of Russian painters. The progressive aspects of his work were continued by among others Surikov, Kramskoy (see No. 36), and Polenov.

Ivanov's early Roman paintings of mythological subjects like *Apollo, Hyacinthus,* and *Zephyrus* (Tretyakov Gallery, Moscow) reveal his ability to paint conventional academic nudes on a heroic scale. However, he soon turned to religious themes. In this field his most notable composition is *Christ Appearing to the People* (Tretyakov Gallery, Moscow) on which he worked for over twenty years, doing innumerable studies after paintings by the Italian masters of the Renaissance, as well as executing several hundred preparatory studies from nature. *Water and Rocks Near Palazzuola* is probably a study for the landscape on the left of this large picture.

This sparkling scene, painted at the shore of Lake Albano near a thirteenth century Franciscan monastery in the Roman *campagna,* where Ivanov often sketched during the 1840's and 50's, displays his skill as a landscape painter and his highly personal sense of color, not unlike that of the Pre-Raphaelites. The painting also has affinities with works by both the German Nazarenes, with whom Ivanov was in contact in Rome, and artists of the Düsseldorf School, who likewise influenced the development of romantic painting in America.

Ivanov's forte was figure painting but his landscapes are interesting in that they reveal how brilliantly he was able to harness a sharp eye for the beauties of nature to a romantic imagination. Here he presents us with a scene that is both literal and idyllic. By closing off the view with a mass of trees, he creates a peaceful sunny domain, into which the onlooker feels readily drawn.

Provenance:
M. P. Botkin, St. Petersburg
The State Russian Museum, Leningrad, 1917

Bibliography:
M. Botkin, *Aleksandr Andreyevich Ivanov, his Life and Correspondence, 1806-1858,* St. Petersburg, 1880.
N. P. Sobko, *Dictionary of Russian Artists,* St. Petersburg, 1895, II, Part I.
Richard Muther, *History of Modern Painting,* 1907, IV, pp. 236-286.
D. Arkin and B. Ternovetz, *Masters of Art on Art,* Moscow, 1937, pp. 117-152.
K. S. Volodina, *On the Subject of the Dating of the Landscapes of Aleksandr Ivanov,* Moscow, 1954.
M. V. Alpatov, *Aleksandr Andreyevich Ivanov, his Life and Work,* Moscow, 1956, I-II.
Aleksandr Andreyevich Ivanov, Catalogue of the Commemorative Exhibition of the 150th Anniversary of his Birth, 1806-1956, Moscow, 1956.
M. V. Alpatov, *Aleksandr Andreyevich Ivanov,* Moscow, 1959.
Moscow Academy of Art, *Aleksandr Andreyevich Ivanov,* Moscow, 1960.
S. G. Muratov, *Aleksandr Ivanov,* Leningrad, 1968.

Exhibitions:
A. A. Ivanov, the 150th Anniversary of his Birth, Tretyakov Gallery, Moscow, 1956.
A. A. Ivanov, the 150th Anniversary of his Birth, The State Russian Museum, Leningrad, 1957, no. 77.

Ivan Konstantinovich Aivazovsky

Theodosia 1817 — Theodosia 1900

35. View of Constantinople by Moonlight 1846
Oil on canvas, 49⅛ x 76⅛ in. (124.7 x 193.2 cm.)
Signed and dated lower right: *Aivazovsky 1846*

Marine painting in nineteenth century Russian art is represented at its best by Aivazovsky. Of Armenian extraction, he grew up in the Crimean town of Theodosia, where from his early youth he was fascinated by the Black Sea. During the years 1833-1839 he studied at the St. Petersburg Academy of Arts, with Vorobyov, but as early as 1835-36 he was already celebrated for his seascapes. Upon leaving the Academy he returned to the Crimea, and in 1840 travelled to Italy, where he met both Gogol and Alexander Ivanov, and painted his huge landscapes: *Storm, Chaos,* and *Neapolitan Night,* which firmly established his reputation. Around 1844 Aivazovsky returned to St. Petersburg, where he was named a member of the Academy and painter to the Admiralty. In St. Petersburg his friends included Briullov, Glinka, Zhukovsky, Krylov, and Pushkin, whose portrait he often painted. Pushkin's lyric passages about the sea are known to have inspired Aivazovsky. In spite of his success in the capital, Aivazovsky decided, in 1845, to leave St. Petersburg and return to Theodosia, where his studio became an important artistic center. In Theodosia he also founded an art school and gallery that still bears his name and contains more than 6,000 of his works. Aivazovsky's early paintings are classical in composition with a marked sensibility for color and light. His later works, those of the seventies and eighties, are almost entirely monochromatic.

This view of Constantinople has always been a favorite with artists and photographers. Aivazovsky may have done sketches on the spot; however, the painting is not entirely correct topographically, so it is more likely to have been executed after the artist returned to Russia from an expedition to Asia Minor and the Greek Islands, led by Admiral F. P. Litke, founder of the Russian Geographical Society. This characteristically picturesque work reveals the artist's romantic feeling for effects of light on water, especially in the way he has bathed the scene in golden moonlight and dappled the channel leading to the Golden Horn with silvery reflections. These light effects enhance the mystery of the oriental city. The dark mass of the Ortaköy mosque—the finest example of Turkish baroque architecture —in the right foreground makes a powerful silhouette against the seraglio section of the old city in the background. The composition is constructed according to traditional principles, with the heavy mass of architecture on the right counter-balancing the expanse of water on the left and the twin sails of the ship echoing the two minarets.

Provenance:
Museum of The Revolution, Leningrad
The State Russian Museum, Leningrad, 1935

Bibliography:
F. I. Bulgakov, *Ivan Konstantinovich Aivazovsky and His Work,* St. Petersburg, 1901.
Y. A. Galabutski, "Aivazovsky in Theodosia (1886-1897)," *Istoricheskij Vestnik,* 97, 104, p. 525.
N. S. Barsamov, *Ivan Konstantinovich Aivazovsky,* Moscow, 1950.
N. S. Barsamov, *Ivan Konstantinovich Aivazovsky,* Moscow, 1958.
N. S. Barsamov, *Ivan Konstantinovich Aivazovsky,* Moscow, 1967.
Ivan Konstantinovich Aivazovsky, Documents and Materials, Erevan, 1967.
N. S. Barsamov, *Aivazovsky in The Crimea,* Simferopol, 1970.

Exhibitions:
Exhibition at the Academy of Arts, St. Petersburg, 1846.
The Works of Ivan Konstantinovich Aivazovsky, Leningrad, 1950.

Ivan Nikolaevich Kramskoy

Ostrogozhsk 1837 — St. Petersburg 1887

36. Portrait of Ivan I. Shishkin 1880
Oil on canvas, 46 x 33½ in. (116.7 x 85.2 cm.)
Signed and dated lower right: *I. Kramskoy 1880*

Kramskoy, who was one of the leaders of the Russian realist movement, worked originally as a retoucher of photographs in Kharkov and St. Petersburg before entering the Academy in 1856. In 1863 he ended his academic career when he initiated the so-called "Mutiny of the 13." Kramskoy and a group of fellow students from the Academy refused to paint the prescribed graduation piece and demanded the right to select subjects taken from everyday life. They resigned from the Academy to create a new group, the *Artel Khudozhnikov* (Artists' Cooperative), which in 1870 became the Society for Traveling Exhibitions (the *Peredvizhniki* or "Wanderers"). Basing their approach on N. Tchernyshevski's revolutionary book, *Aesthetic Relations of Art and Reality* (1855), which stressed the superiority of reality over its representation in art, the "Wanderers" sought to make their work more accessible to the people by concentrating on familiar subjects and sending exhibitions of their works throughout Russia.

Kramskoy was the chief spokesman for the *Peredvizhniki* movement and a prolific painter. His *oeuvre,* with the exception of a few religious works —*e.g. Christ in the Wilderness* (1872, Tretyakov Gallery, Moscow)—consists mostly of portraits. His work often reveals a conflict between the deeply felt mysticism of his ideas and the photographic accuracy of his vision. A somewhat similar combination of mysticism and reportorial accuracy is to be found in the novels of Dostoevsky, whose portrait Kramskoy painted. The artist's photographic technique is most apparent in his portraits, which are rendered with a minute attention to detail, as witness this masterly likeness of Shishkin (1832-1898). Shishkin, also a member of the *Peredvizhniki,* was a talented landscape painter, renowned for his meticulously painted forest scenes. The choice of subject is characteristic. Above all Kramskoy liked to paint well known people—artists, writers, musicians, and intellectuals—whose colorful personalities were a challenge to his almost obsessive concern with physiognomical minutiae.

Kramskoy has depicted Shishkin in a relaxed pose, his hair rather disheveled, his hands in his pockets, and a slightly quizzical expression on his face, as if caught in the midst of a conversation. Although the influence of black-and-white photography is immediately evident, Kramskoy has transcended mere representationalism by conveying the forcefulness of Shishkin's character.

Provenance:
Museum of the Academy of Arts, St. Petersburg,
The State Russian Museum, Leningrad, 1925

References:
Catalogue of the Museum of the Academy of Arts, Russian Painting, St. Petersburg, 1915, no. 1046, pl. p. 117.
The Russian Museum Catalogue, Moscow-Leningrad, 1954, pl. 54.
Guide to the Collections, the Russian Museum, Art of the Second Half of the XIXth Century, Leningrad, 1955, p. 11-12, pl. p. 70.

Additional Bibliography:
D. Arkin and B. Ternovetz, *Masters of Art on Art,* Moscow, 1937, pp. 231-298.
Tretyakov Gallery, *Drawings and Watercolors by V. G. Perov, I. N. Kramskoy and V. V. Vereshchagin,* Moscow, 1955.
N. G. Mashkovtsev, *Ivan Nikolaevich Kramskoy,* Moscow, 1956.
N. G. Mashkovtsev (ed.), "I. Nikolaevich Kramskoy," *Essays on the History of Russian Portrait Painting of the Second Half of the XIXth Century,* Moscow, 1963.
S. N. Goldstein, "I. N. Kramskoy," *History of Russian Art,* I. E. Grabar, ed., Moscow, 1965, IX, Part I.
S. N. Goldstein, *I. N. Kramskoy, His Life and Work,* Moscow, 1965.
Mary Chamot, *Russian Painting,* London, n.d.

Exhibitions:
Eighth Exhibition of the Society for Traveling Art Exhibitions, St. Petersburg and Moscow, 1880.
Commemorative Exhibition of I. N. Kramskoy, St. Petersburg, 1887.
Exhibition for the 100th Anniversary of the Birth of I. N. Kramskoy, Moscow and Leningrad, 1937.
Exhibition of Paintings by Russian and Soviet Artists, London, 1959.

Arkhip Ivanovich Kuinji

Mariupol 1840-43(?) — St. Petersburg 1910

37. Evening in the Ukraine 1878; partly repainted in 1901
Oil on canvas, 33½ x 64⅞ in. (85.2 x 164.7 cm.)

One of Russia's most important landscape painters of the second half of the nineteenth century, Kuinji is celebrated for his lyrical scenes of the Ukranian countryside and his spectacular light effects—scenes at dawn or dusk or by moonlight. Little is known about the artist's early life; he does not seem to have studied art until 1868, when he joined the St. Petersburg Academy of Arts, remaining there until 1874. Kuinji's training at the Academy and the beginning of his independent career coincided with the creation of the Society for Traveling Exhibitions known as *Peredvizhniki* (see note on No. 36). His canvases of this early period are close in spirit to works by members of this group such as Kramskoy, Repin, and the Vasnetsov brothers, with whom he was in close contact and whose ideas influenced his own. They also show the influence of Aivazovsky, whom he considered his master.

Although Kuinji ceased to exhibit around 1882, he remained a prolific painter until his death, working chiefly in St. Petersburg and the Crimea. He was also an active teacher at the Academy, which he joined in 1894. Among his pupils, Rylov, Roerich, and Bogayevsky are the most distinguished. A year before his death he founded an art society (now the Kuinji Society) to which he bequeathed all his works and his property in the Crimea.

Kuinji developed a highly personal style distinguished by a resonant sense of color, bold simplification of form, and an imaginative ability to evoke the atmosphere of a particular place. His light effects are often highly dramatic, and his paint is laid on very heavily, but his pictures are never obvious. What redeems them is the artist's deep response to the richness of nature.

This *Evening in the Ukraine* is one of the first works in Kuinji's mature style. The landscape is built up with a heavy impasto that makes the foliage and thatched roofs almost palpable. And yet the whole scene is bathed in a rosy light that gives an effect of evanescence. Kuinji has admirably caught that poignant moment when the setting sun extracts color from everything and changes trees from green to sepia. The absence of human figures and the movement of shadows across the walls of the deserted white-washed houses further endow the composition with an air of mystery.

Provenance:
Kuinji Society
The Russian Museum of The Emperor
  Alexander III, St. Petersburg, 1914
The State Russian Museum, Leningrad,

References:
Catalogue du musée d'état de l'art Russe,
  Moscow, 1952.
Catalogue of the Russian Museum, Moscow,
  1954, pl. 67.
Guide to the Collection of the Russian Museum,
  Moscow, 1955, p. 33, 78.

Adddditional Bibliography:
M. P. Nevedomsky and I. E. Repin, *Arkhip
  Ivanovich Kuinji,* St. Petersburg, 1913.
M. P. Nevedomsky, *Kuinji,* Moscow, 1937.
N. Novouspensky, *The Russian Museum,
  Painting,* Leningrad, 1974, p. 11.
I. Romanysheva, *Kuinji,* Leningrad, 1975.

Exhibitions:
*Sixth Exhibition of the Society for Traveling
  Art Exhibitions,* St. Petersburg and Kiev,
  1878-1879.
*Russian Art XVIIIth—XXth Centuries, From the
  Collections of the Russian Museum,* Peking-
  Shanghai, 1957-1958.
*Masterpieces of Modern Painting from the
  USSR,* Tokyo and Kyoto, 1966-1967, no. 17.

Ilya Efimovich Repin

Chuguev 1844 — Kuokkala, Finland 1930

38. Portrait of Anton Rubinstein Conducting 1887
Oil on canvas, 40¼ x 33¾ in. (112.2 x 85.7 cm.)
Signed lower right: *I. Rep.*

Repin was the chief exponent of Russian realism and the outstanding Russian painter of the nineteenth century. Although not an original member of the famous "13" (see No. 36), Repin personified their ideals not only in his art but in his philosophy. Born in the Ukraine, he began his study of art in a local school of military topographers and also worked as an icon painter. In 1863 he went to St. Petersburg and entered the School of Design; a year later he joined the Academy of Arts, from which he graduated in 1871. While still a student at the Academy he began his famous picture *The Volga Boatmen* (State Russian Museum), 1870-73, inspired by a visit to the Volga with the landscape painter, Vassiliev, in 1870.

On his graduation Repin received a grant for study abroad. He lived for a time in Paris where he met several compatriots, including Savva Mamontov, who became the most active patron of the arts in Russia when he founded an artists' colony on his estate, Abramtsevo, near Moscow, in 1874. Besides Repin, this colony included Polenov, Serov and later the brothers Vasnetsov, who revived the traditions of Russian folk art in their work. Repin spent several summers at Abramtsevo making studies from nature for use in his paintings. In 1878 he joined the influential *Peredvizhniki* and became a regular contributor to their exhibitions. From 1894-1907 he taught at the Academy; among his students were Serov, Somov, and Anna Ostroumova.

Repin is primarily known for dramatic historical subjects, but he also painted large-scale genre works and portraits, and it is probably in the latter that he is at his best. This *Portrait of Anton Rubinstein Conducting* is one of the finest of a series which includes likenesses of celebrated writers, painters, musicians and governmental figures (notably the sketches of officials for *The Formal Session of the Council of State,* 1903, State Russian Museum)— an invaluable record of the cultural and political life of the time.

Anton Rubinstein (1829-1894) was not only a conductor but a renowned pianist and composer. In 1859 he became the director of the Russian Musical Society, and in 1862 founded the Imperial Conservatory at St. Petersburg. During 1872-73 he made a concert tour through America with the violinist and composer Henryk Wieniawski, playing more than two hundred recitals. Repin painted several portraits of Rubinstein. One of two which the artist began in 1881, this portrait was reworked in 1887, and the figure changed from a seated position to this more dramatic standing pose. Rubinstein is seen conducting, with his right hand about to bring down the baton and the left hand reaching over to turn a page of the score. It is probably no coincidence that Rubinstein's unruly hair and broad face have a Beethoven-like air.

Provenance:
P. D. Yermakov
The State Russian Museum, Leningrad, 1918

Bibliography:
Christian Brinton, *Ilya E. Repin,* London, 1908.
N. S. Morgunov, *I. E. Repin,* Moscow, 1924.
A. Ivanov, *I. E. Repin,* Leningrad, 1925.
S. Ernst, *I. E. Repin,* Leningrad, 1927.
Igor Grabar, *Repin,* Moscow, 1937, 2 Vols.
D. Arkin and B. Ternovetz, *Masters of Art on Art,* Moscow, 1937, pp. 341-416.
D. Rodionovitch, *I. E. Repin, 1844-1930,* Moscow-Leningrad, 1937.
Moscow Academy of Science, *Repin,* Moscow, 1948-1949.
I. S. Silberstein, ed., *I. E. Repin,* Moscow, 1957.
Igor Grabar, Serov and Repin, *Ezhegodnik,* Moscow, 1952, pp. 5-16.
Leningrad Academy of Art, *I. E. Repin: Selected Lectures and Documents,* Moscow, 1952.
V. N. Moskvinov, *Repin in Moscow,* Moscow, 1954.
C. Gray, *The Russian Experiment in Art, 1863-1922,* London, 1962.
O. Lyaskovskaya, *I. E. Repin,* Moscow, 1962.
Igor Grabar, *Repin,* Moscow, 1964, 2 Vols.
D. V. Sarab'yanov, *I. E. Repin, History of Art,* I. E. Grabar, ed., Moscow, 1965, IX, Part I, pp. 445-563.

Exhibitions:
Exhibition of Works by I. E. Repin, Russian Museum, Leningrad, 1925, no. 50.
Paintings of I. E. Repin, Moscow and Leningrad, 1936-1937, no. 208.
Paintings of I. E. Repin, Leningrad, 1958.

Ilya Efimovich Repin

39. Portrait of Tolstoy 1901
Oil on canvas, 80¾ x 28½ in. (205 x 72.5 cm.)
Signed and dated lower left: *I. Repin 1901*

The likenesses of Leo N. Tolstoy (1828-1910) occupy an especially important place among Repin's portraits. The artist met the famous author in 1880, and from then on was a frequent visitor to his estate, Yasnaya Polyana, near Tula. Repin developed a profound admiration for Tolstoy's philosophy and character, and his various portraits convey not only the changing look of the man but his intellectual and spiritual strength.

Repin also catches the inner stresses of Tolstoy's life, as in the well-known portrait of 1887 (Tretyakov Museum, Moscow), showing the writer seated in an armchair with an open book on his knees. There is an air of distinct anxiety about this portrait, which suggests that Tolstoy had not entirely recovered from his spiritual crisis of the late 1870's. This crisis, which had been building up over the previous twenty years, came to a head with Tolstoy's "conversion." He first turned to the orthodox faith, but in 1879 decided to evolve his own form of Christianity based on a doctrine of "non-resistance." This conversion led in 1884 to the writer's unsuccessful attempt to abandon the life of an aristocrat for a peasant existence.

In this almost life-size portrait painted fourteen years later than the Tretyakov picture there is no longer any feeling of strain. Basing himself on a study from life and a bust he had made in 1891, Repin effectively conveys the genius, resignation and sanctity of the writer in old age. Hence the air of pensive concentration in the face and pose, particularly in the way Tolstoy's large hands are thoughtfully tucked into his belt. In keeping with his attempt to lead a simple life, the writer is depicted barefoot and wearing a plain peasant shirt—the white *rubashka* held together with a leather belt. In his pocket is a red-bound book, probably the Bible which was always with him in his later years.

Despite the simplicity and informality in keeping with Tolstoy's back-to-nature theories, there is a monumental quality to this portrait, which is emphasized by the verticality of the composition. There is also a sense of isolation—the writer is seemingly unaware of the artist—which reflects the loneliness of Tolstoy's genius. Far from being a decorative backdrop contrived in the studio, the setting is a convincing forest scene painted with all of Repin's freshness and assurance—an appropriate habitat for this prophet who had become one of the most venerated men in the world.

Provenance:
Collection of the artist
The Russian Museum of The Emperor
    Alexander III, St. Petersburg, 1901
The State Russian Museum, Leningrad,

References:
Igor Graber, *Repin*, Moscow, 1964, II, pl.
    facing p. 52.

Additional Bibliography:
N. Mashkovtsev, *L. N. Tolstoy in the Works of
    I. E. Repin*, Moscow-Leningrad, 1948.
I. E. Repin and Lev N. Tolstoy, *Correspondence*
    (2 volumes), Moscow, 1949.
A. Zotov, *L. N. Tolstoy in the Paintings of
    Russian Artists*, Moscow, 1953.

Exhibitions:
Works of I. E. Repin, The State Russian Museum,
    Leningrad, 1925.
Paintings by I. E. Repin, Moscow, 1935,
    Leningrad, 1937.
*Works by I. E. Repin Portraying the Life and
    Work of L. N. Tolstoy,* Tokyo-Osaka,
    1966-1967, Czechoslovakia, 1967-1968.
L. N. Tolstoy and his Contemporaries, Museum
    of L. N. Tolstoy, Moscow, 1968-1973.

Isaac Ilyich Levitan

Kibarty 1860 — Moscow 1900

40. Silence 1898
Oil on canvas, 38 x 50⅞ in. (96.7 x 129.2 cm.)
Signed lower right: *I. Levitan*

Levitan's art developed out of the traditions of the previous generation, notably the lyrical landscape idiom of his teacher, Aleksei Savrassov (1830-1887), "the father of Russian landscape painting." The artist received his training from 1873 until 1884, at the Moscow School of Painting, Sculpture and Architecture not only with Savrassov but also with the dynamic teacher V. D. Polenov (1844-1927), who introduced him to Savva Mamontov's artists' colony at Abramtsevo. In 1889 he visited Paris, where he was greatly impressed by the Barbizon school.

Through his association with Mamontov, Levitan became involved in designing and painting scenery for theatrical performances. At first somewhat amateurish, these productions ultimately became highly professional, and as "The Private Opera" were much admired by the Moscow intelligentsia. Mamontov's theatrical experiments had important consequences: they inspired Diaghilev to use *avant garde* artists for his décors; they gave Stanislavsky, Mamontov's cousin, his first experience of the stage; and they showed Levitan and other artists who worked on the sets how to simplify the natural scene and endow it with an element of drama. With a few adjustments, many of Levitan's landscapes could serve as settings for the plays of Anton Chekhov, with whom the artist has often been compared.

From 1884 onwards Levitan exhibited with the *Peredvizhniki* (see notes on Nos. 36 and 37), but he did not join their *Society of the Traveling Exhibitions* until 1891. In 1886 he embarked on a two year trip on the Volga which had significant repercussions on his style. After this trip his painting became even more lyrical, yet always remained rooted in reality. Simple in form, subtle in handling and profound in their feeling for nature, Levitan's late works—*peysagy nastroyenia* (mood landscapes)—are among the glories of Russian nineteenth century painting.

In its haunting clarity, *Silence* is a characteristic example of Levitan's late style. Always a master at rendering the subtle play of Russian light, the artist has caught the particular stillness of *l'heure bleue,* the twilight hour, in the country, when the slightest noise makes silence seem the heavier. With its sliver of a moon, this is indeed a "mood landscape." The endless stretch of the Russian plain, the dark thatched huts, the ominous forest and the absence of humanity give further credence to the title. As the Russian critic, N. Novouspensky has written, Levitan's landscapes "reflect a state of mind . . . they are poems about the motherland in all its natural beauty and majestic grandeur."

Provenance:
The State Russian Museum, Leningrad, 1927

References:
S. Glagol and I. Grabar, *Isaac I. Levitan, His Life and Work,* Moscow, 1922, p. 94.
A. Fedorov-Davydov, ed., *I. I. Levitan—Letters, Documents, Reminiscences,* Moscow, 1956, facing p. 177.
Konstantin Paustovski, *Isaac Levitan,* Dresden, 1965, pl. 43.

Bibliography:
I. Ginzburg, *I. Levitan,* Leningrad & Moscow, 1937.
I. I. Levitan (Album), Tretyakov Gallery, Moscow, 1938.
V. Kostin, *I. I. Levitan,* Moscow, 1938.
V. A. Prytkov, *Chekhov and Levitan,* Moscow, 1948.
Janina Ruszczyc, *Levitan,* Warsaw, 1957.
V. A. Prytkov, *I. I. Levitan,* Moscow, 1960.
T. Yurova, *I. I. Levitan,* Moscow, 1960.
F. C. Maltseva, "I. I. Levitan and Landscape Painting of the 1890's," in *History of Russian Painting,* Moscow, 1965, X, Part I, pp. 108-138.

Exhibitions:
Mir Iskusstva, St. Petersburg, 1899, no. 138.
Exposition de l'Art russe, Salon d'Automne, Paris, 1906, no. 271.
Russische Kunst, Berlin, 1906-07, no. 224.
All-Russian Exhibition of the Works of I. I. Levitan, Moscow, 1938, no. 259; Leningrad, 1939, no. 178.
A Retrospective of the Works of I. I. Levitan, Leningrad, 1961 *(hors catalogue).*

Valentin Aleksandrovich Serov

St. Petersburg 1865 — Moscow 1911

41. Portrait of Maria Federovna Morozova 1897
Oil on canvas, 43 x 34⅞ in. (109.2 x 88.7 cm.)
Signed and dated below center left: *Serov 97.*

Serov came from a cultivated family, both his father and mother being distinguished musicians. After the death of his father in 1874 the boy was taken by his mother to Rome. There he received drawing lessons from Repin, and even more important, met that most creative of Russian patrons, Savva Mamontov—"singer, sculptor, stage director, dramatist," according to Camilla Gray—who invited the mother and son to join the artists' colony he had formed on his estate, Abramtsevo, near Moscow. Serov thus grew up in the most progressive atmosphere that existed in Russia at the time. Later he studied at the St. Petersburg Academy, again with his old friend Repin, also in P. Chystiakov's studio, where he worked side-by-side with the brilliant young artist, Mikhail Vrubel whose mythological compositions in a flamboyant style were to have a profound impact on the development of modern Russian art. Leaving the Academy in 1885, Serov travelled extensively in western Europe.

On his return Serov soon became the most brilliant and sought after portraitist in the country—"the Russian Menzel." In 1895 he was nominated to the St. Petersburg Academy and, in 1897, appointed professor at the Moscow School of Painting, Sculpture and Architecture. Apart from portraits, many of them of the Imperial Family and the court, Serov painted a wide range of subjects including landscapes, historical compositions and, at the end of his life, décors for Diaghilev's *Ballets Russes*. A superb master of many techniques, Serov was also a protean artist capable of painting bravura portraits, *e.g.* the one of O. Orlova (State Russian Museum), which are as elegant as Boldini's. He was also master of a spare expressive manner, *e.g. Portrait of Ida Rubinstein* of 1910 (State Russian Museum), that has parallels with Munch and Schiele.

"Utterly simple and direct, but of a consummate craftsmanship," Alexandre Benois' comment on Serov's portraits certainly applies to this one of the matriarch of the Morozovs, a prominent Moscow family of merchants and collectors. Maria Federovna (1829-1911) was the mother of Savva Morozov, a founder of the Moscow Art Theater and a forebear of Ivan A. Morozov, the famous collector of nineteenth and twentieth century French painting, with whom Serov visited Paris in the early years of the century to advise him on his art purchases, notably the acquisition of two major van Goghs. The artist has portrayed the old woman in a dignified pose, yet he also conveys her motherly warmth. She seems to have just removed her spectacles, and her good left eye has a keen sparkle as it gazes knowingly out at us. This and the *brio* with which her headdress is painted takes the stiffness out of a potentially intimidating image.

Provenance:
Tretyakov Gallery, Moscow
The State Russian Museum, Leningrad, 1934

References:
N. E. Radlov, *Serov,* St. Petersburg, 1911.
M. Kovalensky, *Valentin Serov, étude sur sa vie et son oeuvre,* Brussels, 1913.
I. Grabar, *Valentin Aleksandrovich Serov, His Life and Work,* Moscow, 1913.
Alesandre Benois, *The Russian School of Painting,* New York, 1916, pp. 165-7.
S. Ernst, *Valentin A. Serov,* Leningrad, 1921.
S. Makovsky, *Valentin Serov,* Berlin, 1922.
D. Arkin and B. Ternovetz, *Masters of Art on Art,* Moscow, 1937, pp. 499-520.
Valentin A. Serov, Correspondence, 1884-1911, Leningrad, Moscow, 1937.
I. Grabar, "Serov and Repin," *Ezhegodnik,* Moscow, 1952, pp. 5-16.
C. Gray, *The Russian Experiment in Art, 1863-1922,* London, 1962, pp. 27-29.
G. S. Arbuzov, *Valentin Serov, Portrait Painting,* Leningrad, 1968.
I. S. Silberstein and V. A. Samkov, eds., *Valentin Serov in Reminiscences, Journals and Correspondence of His Contemporaries,* I, part 2, Leningrad, 1971.

Exhibitions:
XVIIth Periodical Exhibition of the Moscow Society of the Arts, Moscow, 1897.
XXVI Exhibition of the Society for Traveling Art Exhibitions, St. Petersburg, 1898.
Commemorative Exhibition of the Works by Valentin A. Serov, St. Petersburg, 1914.
Paintings by Valentin A. Serov, Leningrad, Moscow, 1935.
Works of Valentin A. Serov, Moscow, 1958-59, Kiev, 1959, Leningrad, 1959-60.
100th Anniversary of the Birth of Valentin Aleksandrovich Serov, (1865-1911), Moscow, 1965, Leningrad, 1966.
Portrait Painting of the "Peredvizhniki," Moscow, Leningrad, Kiev, 1972.

Konstantin Andreyevich Somov

St. Petersburg 1869 — Paris 1939

42. Portrait of Anna Petrovna Ostroumova 1901
Oil on canvas, 38⅝ x 25⅝ in. (98 x 65.2 cm.)
Signed and dated upper left: *K. Somov, 1901*

A brilliant portrait and landscape painter, book illustrator, and theatrical designer, Somov was born into the St. Petersburg intelligentsia. His father was a well-known art historian and curator at the Hermitage. By the age of ten, Somov was already a skilled draughtsman, but it was not until 1888 that he entered the St. Petersburg Academy of Arts. In 1894 he began studying with Repin. During his years as a student, Somov made two trips to Italy, and after graduating from the Academy, went to Paris. There he joined a circle of young expatriate artists that included Bakst, Benois, Lanceray and Ostroumova, the subject of this portrait. Somov developed an infatuation for French art and poetry, made frequent trips to Versailles, and studied the paintings of Watteau, Largillière, and the eighteenth century French portraitists. However, his taste was truly eclectic, and the art of Chardin, Poussin, de Hoogh, Japanese print-makers, as well as of contemporaries like Conder and members of the *Simplicissimus* group also influenced his work.

Somov's stylized genre scenes which owe a debt to Watteau's *Cythera* are almost decadent in their elegance. Benois refers to these works as "excessively spiced, suffocatingly perfumed, over-refined and morbidly delicate." And yet, like fellow members of the *Nevsky Pickwickians* and *Mir Iskusstva* (World of Art) groups, Somov must be counted among the pioneers of the modernist movement in Russia, whose work helped to open up their country to western ideas, in the same way that their participation in Diaghilev's exhibition of Russian painting at the *Salon d'Automne* in 1906 familiarized the West with contemporary developments in Russian art. The 1906 exhibition revealed that the *Mir Iskusstva* group had affinities with the French *Nabis*—artists like Bonnard and Vuillard.

As Benois wrote: "Somov's art is steeped in quiet sadness and skepticism. It is all impregnated with the mysterious power of inspiration and divination, but at the same time there is a note of despair in it . . . He had a consummate perfection of technique, a perfection unknown to the whole of Russian painting of the second half of the nineteenth century."

In his many portraits Somov displays a less *fin de siècle* sensibility than in his genre scenes. This pensive yet radiant work represents the gifted artist Anna P. Ostroumova-Lebiedieva (1871-1955), a student of Repin and later (1898-99) of Whistler at the *Académie Carmen* in Paris. Like Somov, she was a member of the *Mir Iskusstva* group; she was also the author of an autobiographical journal which provides an invaluable account of Russian art at the turn of the century. Ostroumova later became a professor at the Academy and remained an active artist in the U.S.S.R. until her death.

Provenance:
Collection of A. P. Ostroumova-Lebiedieva,
    St. Petersburg
The State Russian Museum, Leningrad, 1956

Bibliography:
Oscar Bie, *Constantin Somoff,* Berlin, 1907.
Alexandre Benois, *The Russian School of Painting,* New York, 1916, p. 1863.
S. Ernst, *Somov,* St. Petersburg, 1918.
E. V. Zhuravleva, *Konstantin Andreyevich Somov: Essays on Russian Portrait Painting at the End of the XIXth-Beginning XXth Century,* XIII, Moscow, 1964.
Irina Pruzhan, *Konstantin Somov,* Moscow, 1972.

Exhibitions:
Mir Iskusstva, St. Petersburg, 1902.
Exhibition of Paintings, Sketches and Drawings by Konstantin Somov, St. Petersburg, Berlin, Hamburg, 1903.
Exhibition of Russian Painting XVIIIth-Beginning XXth Century from Private Collections in Leningrad, Leningrad, 1955.
Hundredth Anniversary of the birth of Konstantin Andreyevich Somov, Leningrad, 1969-1970, Moscow, 1970.
Portrait Painting in Russian Art at the End of the XIXth-Beginning XXth Century, Leningrad, 1975.

Léon Samoylovich Bakst

Grodno 1866 — Paris 1924

43. Portrait of Sergei Diaghilev with his Nurse 1906
Oil on canvas, 63⅞ x 46½ in. (162.2 x 118.2 cm.)
Signed and dated lower left: *L. Bakst 1906*

Born Lev Rosenberg, Bakst entered the St. Petersberg Academy of Arts when he was seventeen, only to be dismissed eighteen months later for unconventional behavior. He subsequently studied under the Finnish painter Albert Edelfeldt (1854-1905). In 1890 Bakst joined Alexandre Benois' *Nevsky Pickwickians,* and met the young dilettante, Sergei Diaghilev (1872-1929). Diaghilev and Bakst were drawn together by the fact that other members regarded them as outsiders: Diaghilev, because he was an uncultivated snob from the provinces, and Bakst, because he was the only Jew in the group, "a clerk out of a Gogol short story" (Charles Spencer). For some time neither was taken very seriously, but their energy and persistence was soon rewarded. In the mid-1890's Bakst went to Paris where he received his first major commission: a vast historical composition for the Grand Duke Vladimir Alexandrovitch. Back in St. Petersburg, he had success with his society portraits. Meanwhile, Diaghilev launched a magazine called *Mir Iskusstva (World of Art)* and sponsored a group of artists including Bakst and Benois. The first number, handsomely produced if somewhat precious, appeared in November, 1898; it was followed by an exhibition of contemporary Russian art under the auspices of *Mir Iskusstva.*

Diaghilev's apartment doubled as an office, and Bakst worked as illustrator, photographic retoucher, and general factotum. There were constant rows and reconciliations until 1904, when the magazine failed for lack of funds. Bakst continued to contribute to other new Russian publications like *The Golden Fleece,* which devoted an issue to him in 1906. Meanwhile he had made his debut as a theatrical designer with *Le Coeur de la Marquise* (1902), a mime devised by Marius Petipa for the Tsar's private theater in the Hermitage. A year later his décor for *"La Fée des Poupées"* was acclaimed by the public. Bakst also did settings for Diaghilev's lavish exhibition of Russian portraits in 1905 (St. Petersburg) and his show of Russian painting at the 1906 *Salon d'Automne* (Paris).

The present portrait commemorates this close collaboration. Bakst has depicted his arrogant mentor with affection, tinged by mockery. In the background Diaghilev's self-effacing old *nyanya* sets off the dandified young impressario with the distinctive white streak in his hair. Diaghilev must already have realized that the *Mir Iskusstva* movement was too provincial to win him international fame, so he reverted to his first love, music. The opera company, featuring Chaliapin in *Boris Godounov,* that he took to Paris in 1908 had a triumph. But it was not until he returned to Paris in 1909 with the *Ballets Russes* that Diaghilev discovered his true forte: the rest of his life was identified with the ballet. The colorful décors that Bakst provided for ballets like *Schehérézade* (1910) contributed enormously to the worldwide success of the *Ballets Russes* and launched a craze for exotic colors and patterns that affected most of the applied arts.

Provenance:
The State Russian Museum, Leningrad

Bibliography:
Martin Birnbaum, *Léon Bakst,* New York, 1919.
André Levinson, *Bakst, The Story of the Artist's Life.* London, 1923.
André Levinson, *The Designs of Léon Bakst for the Sleeping Princess.* London, 1923.
André Levinson, *Bakst.* Paris, 1924.
Louis Réau, *Unpublished Works of Bakst.* New York, 1927.
A. Haskell, *Diagileff—His Artistic and Private Life.* London, 1935.
Raymond Lister, *The Moscovite Peacock: A Study of the Art of Léon Bakst,* Mortlocks, Meldreth, 1954.
C. Gray, *The Russian Experiment in Art 1863-1922.* London, 1962, pp. 17-64.
Valentine Marcade, *Le renouveau dans l'art picturale russe, 1863-1914.* Lausanne, 1971, pp. 83-123.
Charles Spencer, *Léon Bakst.* London, 1973.

Exhibitions:
Mir Iskusstva, St. Petersburg, 1906.
Exposition de l'art russe, Salon d'Automne, Paris and Berlin, 1906-1907.
Exhibition of Russian Portrait Painting XVIIIth— Beginning XXth Century, Leningrad, 1959.
Portrait Painting in Russian Art from the End of the XIXth—Beginning of the XXth Century, Leningrad, 1975.

131

Index of Artists

Credits

Catalogue design by Joseph del Gaudio Design Group Inc., New York, N.Y.

Set in Times Roman regular and bold by Quad Typographers, Inc., New York, N.Y.

Printed by Colorcraft Offset Inc., New York, N.Y.